STORIES OF INSIGHT AND INSPIRATION

Compiled by
MARGIE CALHOUN JENSEN

BOOKCRAFT, INC.
Salt Lake City, Utah

Library of Congress Catalog Card Number: 76-5174

ISBN 0-88494-296-1

First Printing, 1976

LITHOGRAPHED IN U.S.A BY
PUBLISHERS PRESS
SALT LAKE CITY UTAH

PREFACE

Like its companion volume *When Faith Writes the Story,* this is a book of testimonies. Since the Spirit works in varied areas of our lives, the testimonies or stories are here classified by subject, first throughout the book and then in an index (following the contents pages) which places the accounts in overlapping as well as in main topics. This feature will facilitate ready location of stories on desired topics.

Nothing we possess is so precious as our testimony of the gospel. Like love, this testimony becomes more beautiful and precious as we impart it to others. Not that one can *give* a testimony to someone else, no matter how much he would desire to. President Joseph F. Smith reminds us that "testimony is a personal possession; one cannot give a testimony to another, yet he is able to aid his earnest brother in gaining a true testimony for himself." Clearly, all of us can gain strength, knowledge, and faith from shared spiritual experiences.

I express my appreciation for those faithful Latter-day Saints who have agreed to share their beautiful faith-promoting experiences through this volume. May I join with them in expressing the hope that this book will in some small way assist those who read it to attain a greater understanding of the gospel and a greater faith in our Heavenly Father.

I express appreciation also to George Bickerstaff, Bookcraft's editor, for his capable guidance and sincere interest. Most of all, I am grateful to my husband, Marc, for his never-failing support and encouragement.

CONTENTS

SUBJECT INDEX

(Main Section references shown in italics)

BAPTISM

There is but one way in which men can receive salvation, exaltation and glory, and that is through the order of baptism and the ordinances connected therewith. No mortal man or woman will ever receive celestial glory unless he or she has been baptized, receiving this ordinance personally or by proxy. That is the order that God has established.

—Lorenzo Snow, *Deseret Weekly News,*
54:482, March 13, 1897

ANSWERS FROM THE LORD
Heinrich Stilger

It was in October of 1965 that two young men knocked on the door of my apartment in Frankfurt, Germany. They introduced themselves as missionaries from The Church of Jesus Christ of Latter-day Saints and indicated that they would like to discuss the teachings of their church with me.

At first I did not want to talk to them because the day before I had had a long discussion with some people from another church, which I found intellectually intriguing. But something forced me to listen to these two young boys. I can't explain the feeling I had, but it was as though some kind of radio message came to me that I should listen to their message, so I invited them in and listened as they sincerely and simply presented some of the doctrines of their church. The concepts they presented were decidedly different, yet quite logical, so I agreed to an appointment wherein they would further explain the teachings of their church.

Unfortunately, before the date of our next discussion arrived, I was suddenly hospitalized. I therefore assumed that that was the end of my discussions with the Mormon missionaries, but they actually came to the hospital to see me and continued to give me the discussions in my hospital room. I was quite impressed with the dedication of these young men, and with their message of the restoration of the true Church, so it was not long before I agreed to their request that I set a date for my baptism.

As that date drew closer, I began to question my decision to be baptized. I had always been a heavy smoker and, as is common with most Germans, I did enjoy drinking the excellent wines and beer that my country has to offer. I therefore found the Word of Wisdom very difficult to live, and I was also not fully convinced about tithing, so I cancelled the plans for my baptism and put the missionaries off whenever they suggested another date. My wife was baptized on schedule, but I found myself pulling further and further away from the Church. The missionaries continued to work with me to prepare me so that I could accept another baptismal date, but I was not convinced that I *could* live the Word of Wisdom, or that I *should* be living the Word of Wisdom.

Months went by, and I continued to resist the elders' efforts to bring me into the Church. My wife seemed to have a new-found sense of inner peace, but I became increasingly more bewildered and unhappy with myself as time went by. The missionaries were patient with me, but they were transferred without bringing me to a conviction that the Word of Wisdom was inspired doctrine.

Some time later, another elder came to visit me, and somehow he was able to awaken that same feeling I had had at first with the other elders. He taught me slowly and guided me back over the principles of the gospel. Then, during one of our discussions I read in John 16:23 where Jesus said, "Verily, verily, I say unto you, Whatsoever ye shall ask the Father in my name, he will give it you."

This young elder then counselled me to do just exactly what we have been told to do in the scriptures—pray to our Father in heaven and ask him if the gospel is true. I desperately needed to know the truth, so I accepted the elder's admonition to pray about it. That evening I knelt down and asked my Heavenly Father for forgiveness and for a knowledge of the truthfulness of the teachings of the Church, especially the Word of Wisdom and tithing. I prayed, expecting an answer that I had been told in the scriptures that I would receive, but nothing happened.

I still needed some answers that I knew could come only from the Lord, so I prayed again the next night and pleaded with the Lord for a knowledge of the truth. And then, a bright figure suddenly appeared before me and in rather definite and certain tones addressed me, saying, "The Word of Wisdom and tithing are commandments of God!" Without further comment, he departed.

There may be those who will scoff when I say that I saw an angel, but I *did*—just as surely as the Prophet Joseph Smith saw the angel Moroni. I have no doubts that I was visited by a messenger of the Lord, or that the Word of Wisdom and tithing are commandments of God.

After this soul-stirring experience, it was a simple matter for me to stop smoking and drinking, and this time *I* asked the elders to set a date for my baptism, which I kept.

> Originally reported in "His Testimony Came Through Prayer," *Church News,* January 17, 1970, p. 6.

I WANT TO BE A MORMON

William Henry Bowen III

My early years of growing up in Rochester, New York, were filled with a longing to visit the West. The opportunity for that dream to come true occurred three years ago during my summer vacation.

The family eagerly began making plans for our vacation to Cape Cod. Everyone, that is, but me. I'd been to Cape Cod before and had enjoyed it tremendously, but my idea of the perfect vacation was taking a trip down the Colorado River and shooting the rapids. After some discussion on the matter of where we should vacation, it was decided that my family would go to Cape Cod and I would travel alone to Utah and take my long-dreamed-of river trip.

The trip down the Colorado was as exciting as I had dreamed it would be, and more. In fact, I had such a good time that I decided to stay for another week and see more of the sights before returning east.

I went to Salt Lake City and spent a few days with a friend, just enjoying motorcycling and the impressive mountain scenery. Thursday of that week came and I'd seen much of the natural scenery, but I hadn't visited any of the usual tourist attractions that I really should see before I left. The first place every tourist in Salt Lake City wants to visit is Temple Square, so that was first on my agenda.

It was such a dramatic contrast to leave the bustling city streets of Salt Lake and to walk onto the temple grounds. Everything was so serene and beautiful. I thoroughly enjoyed just wandering around the beautifully landscaped grounds, visiting the historic Tabernacle, and browsing through the museum and looking at all of the artifacts of Mormon history and culture.

I then joined a tour and we entered the Visitors Center. I was quite impressed with the displays, which were beautifully done, informative, and very interesting. The tour director then ushered us into a small theater where we viewed the film, "Man's Search for Happiness." Tears came to my eyes as the beautiful plan of salvation was portrayed on the screen. Something within me said that the beautiful concepts about our eternal existence and the purpose of our life here on earth were true. But, I wondered, why is this doctrine not taught by my church? Why is it taught only by the Mormon Church?

I was so impressed and touched by this experience that when the tour ended, I decided to go back to the Visitors Center on my own. As I approached the east side of the building I noticed a guest book. Suddenly, a stream of light descended from above and rested on the guest book! I walked over to the book and as I looked up, I saw a heavenly figure smiling down upon me and then I heard the words, "Sign it, for it will do you good!"

I signed my name and address, and then in the comment section I wrote, "I want to be a Mormon!" And, at the same time, I said those words out loud. As soon as I had written those words and said them out loud a warm, burning feeling began growing within me. I repeated the words, "I want to be a Mormon!" the second time louder and more intense than before. As I did so, that feeling inside me grew even more intense and seemed to be overpowering me. I didn't understand what was happening—I thought I was having a heart attack! I had never experienced the workings of the Spirit and the Holy Ghost before, so I assumed that there had to be something physically wrong with me.

I looked up and though the light and the heavenly figure were gone, the warm, glowing feeling continued to stay with me. I decided then that I really should know more about this church that I had said I wanted to join. So I went downstairs and took one of each of the free pamphlets that were offered and purchased a Book of Mormon for fifty cents.

I hurried back to my motel room, sat down, and read all of the pamphlets and started to read the Book of Mormon. I read late into the evening and came to the conclusion that what I had said while standing by that guest book at the Visitors Center was true—I *did* want to be a Mormon!

I left Salt Lake City the next day at noon and arrived in Rochester at 5:30 that evening. As soon as I was inside the house, I dropped my bags and went to the telephone and called the missionaries. "How fast can I be baptized?" I asked. "When and where can I be baptized, and do they have a Mormon Church that I can go to when I go back to college?" I blurted out.

"Slow down for just a minute," the missionary said. "Can we come and see you and discuss all this with you?"

"Well, my parents aren't home, so perhaps it would be best if I didn't entertain anyone while they are gone," I replied.

"Would you like to come and see us then?" the missionary asked.

"Certainly!"

I met with the elders the next day at their apartment and started the missionary lessons. I continued meeting with them twice a week, and three weeks later they agreed that I was then properly prepared to be baptized.

I had been eagerly looking forward to the day when I would be baptized into the Church—until that day arrived. Instead of being excited and happy about my baptism, I was depressed. I felt so strange. I knew that the Church was true and that I was doing the right thing, but I felt as if I could not go through with it. I was ill, and even blacked out for a few moments. But, ill or not,

I decided I was going to be baptized anyway! As soon as I made that commitment, most of my physical discomfort began to subside and I began to feel much better. However, I was still uneasy about everything, so I called the missionaries to make sure that everything was proceeding as we had planned. They replied that the font already had been filled, all the arrangements had been completed, and everything was ready and waiting.

I relaxed somewhat and drove over to the chapel, but found that there wasn't any water in the font. Someone had inadvertently emptied it.

The elders asked me to come back again that evening, which I did, and this time the font was filled. I excitedly changed into my white clothing to prepare for my baptism. I was finally going to be a Mormon! But just as soon as I approached the font, that same strange feeling that I had experienced earlier in the day returned. I became terribly uncomfortable and then violently ill within just a few seconds. The missionaries told me that I could be baptized at a later time when I felt better, but I said, "No! I'm going to be baptized—today. I'm not going to let the devil stop me."

As soon as I entered the water, the dark, depressing, ill feelings left me. Since I was baptized a member of the Church, I've known only the greatest feelings of joy and happiness.

Since my baptism on August 26, 1972, I have wondered about the reason for my having received a special witness that the Church is true. Not all converts have seen a light descend from heaven or have seen a heavenly personage. Why then should I have been chosen for this choice blessing? I've never deluded myself with the thought that I have been foreordained and guided to come into the Church to assume high office and perform a great and marvelous work. But then, if this was not the purpose for the heavenly manifestation, what was the reason?

I feel reasonably assured that I found the answer to that question when I became acquainted with an article in the June 1959 *Improvement Era* in which Patriarch to the Church Eldred G. Smith stated in a conference address:

"This is your responsibility, brothers and sisters, to make sure that your genealogy is gathered. I see the effects of this spirit of Elijah becoming stronger all the time. Often it is just one member of the family who joins the Church. I have many husbands and wives come to me, each one being the only member of the Church in his immediate family. I believe the Lord deliberately designates and sends a valiant spirit into a special family in a special location, even in far-off missions, for the explicit purpose of having a spirit who will accept of the gospel of Jesus Christ, hear the voice when it comes to him and recognize it as true. Then, after becoming a member of the Church, he will gather the records, that the promises to the fathers may be fulfilled. Many people who join the Church are the only ones in their family in the Church and are especially assigned and their special mission is to gather their genealogy and perform the sealing blessings that the fathers may receive the blessings promised in the promise of Elijah."

I am the only member of my family that has accepted the gospel, and has received the spirit of Elijah. I am consumed with a burning desire to search out the records of my departed kindred so that I might bring to them the same blessings that I now enjoy by having been baptized into the Church. I know that my great mission in life is to complete the genealogical records of those that have gone before me.

I realized my boyhood dream to go out west and shoot the rapids of the Colorado. But I now have a greater dream—to complete the work for all my departed kindred so that someday we may all be together in the celestial kingdom.

HE WANTS YOU TO BE BAPTIZED
Julia Palazuelos

Every now and then some tall young *gringos* dressed in white shirts, black pants and ties would come to our little town of Guasave in Sinaloa, Mexico. They were different, so the children in the village took great delight in teasing the Mormon missionaries. No one in the village, including me, was particularly interested in his own religion, much less the strange doctrines that were taught by these strange-looking Americans.

Then one day two young American girls came to Guasave, knocked on my door, and greeted me with, "Hi, Julia! How are you?"

I was very surprised at this, and wondered how these Americans could possibly have known my name. They were friendly and seemed sincere enough so I invited them in. They explained that they were Mormon missionaries and had taught the gospel to my brother and sister who were living in Guadalajara. They told me that my brother and sister were going to be baptized and they had requested that the missionaries come to Guasave to teach me the gospel. The lady missionaries then asked if they could come back another time and teach me about the Mormon Church. They were so enthusiastic, and I couldn't see any harm in it, so I agreed.

After about a month and four or five lessons about the Church, they asked me if I was ready to be baptized.

"I don't really know if I should or not," I replied.

"Well then," Sister Sommers said, "what you should do is pray about it and ask your Heavenly Father if you should be baptized."

I didn't know how to pray—I had never prayed before! There wasn't a church or a priest to teach us about God in our little village, so the people in Guasave were not accustomed to praying for guidance on spiritual matters.

"Tonight, Julia," Sister Sommers advised, "after everyone is asleep, kneel down by your bed and ask your Heavenly Father if he wants you to be baptized."

Our home is very modest by North American standards— two rooms (a living room and one bedroom for the entire family). So, after everyone was asleep, I got out of my bed, knelt down, and humbly asked God if I should be baptized into the Mormon Church.

I waited and nothing happened, so I went back to bed. Well, so much for the principle of prayer, I thought.

I soon fell asleep and had a very strange dream. I saw a large room filled with people who were excitedly talking among themselves and saying, "There he is! Let's follow him!" I opened the door to this room, entered, and all the people disappeared except for one man who appeared to be about fifty or sixty feet away. He had long hair and a white beard and wore the brightest white robe I have ever seen. He carried a large staff, and was actually standing about six inches off the floor! I could feel his powerful eyes looking at me and penetrating my very being, even though

I couldn't see his eyes or any detail of his face. His clothing was distinct, but I couldn't see one feature of his face!

"Come, follow me!" he said.

His voice was so kindly, yet commanding, that I followed after him. Immediately we began climbing a very high mountain— one I had never seen, for there are no mountains in this part of Mexico. He continued to climb up the mountain and I began to feel an almost consuming desire to follow after him and to touch him. But no matter how hard I tried, I could not get close enough to him to reach out and touch him. I found it extremely difficult to climb that mountain, while he did so easily and seemingly without effort.

Climbing this steep mountain was so very hard, but I continued to follow after him. I never looked back, but kept my eyes on him and followed in his footsteps. Finally I reached the top of the mountain and suddenly he was no longer there!

The dream ended and suddenly I was very much awake and very confused by what had happened. I couldn't go back to sleep. I spent the rest of the night rehearsing this strange dream in my mind and wondering what it meant.

I waited anxiously for morning and the missionaries to come. This time, two of the elders came by. I related my dream to them and asked them if they knew what it meant. One of the elders then excitedly exclaimed, "Julia, *He* wants you to be baptized!"

I no longer hesitated. I was baptized later that afternoon. Since that day, I have continued to grow in my love and understanding of the Church.

For several years I continued to wonder about that dream I had the night before my baptism. I didn't understand why I was unable to see the Savior's face when the rest of his features and clothing were so distinct and clear. Then, about a year ago, I received the answer to that question when I attended a conference that was held in Arizona. In his address, President Spencer W. Kimball stated that we would not be permitted to look upon the Savior's face if we were not worthy. He then challenged the youth of the Church to set their lives in order and prepare themselves for eternal life in the celestial kingdom where they would be privileged to dwell with our beloved Savior and look upon his face.

This great blessing is granted only to the pure in heart, and I had not been found worthy. However, since I had that dream, I have tried to follow in the Savior's footsteps. My great desire now is to live a righteous life and prepare for that day when, hopefully, I will be counted worthy to enter the celestial kingdom and gaze upon the Savior's face.

Originally reported in *Church News,* February 24, 1973, p. 13.

ONE DAY ONLY

George C. Lambert

Niels P. L. Eskildz was born May 31, 1836, at Lindholm, County of Aalborg, Denmark, only a few miles from the city of Aalborg, which is celebrated as being the birthplace of President Anthon H. Lund. The parents of Niels were unassuming country folks, with nothing to distinguish them from their industrious and respectable neighbors except their rather unusual size and a certain pride of bearing and correctness of speech due to their superior education, and the fact that they were both descendants in a direct line from noble, titled families.

Niels was the youngest of the family, having two brothers of almost gigantic stature and a sister who, when grown, was the largest woman in that part of Denmark. Niels also would doubtless have grown to be an unusually large man had he not met with an awful accident when ten years of age.

Denmark is a country almost without fences, the farms being separated one from another by imaginary lines. Instead of the cows and sheep owned by the farmers being allowed to range at will in pastures, the custom was and still is to stake them out individually, and lead them in at night. As a rule, the cows are models of decorum, and one of the prettiest as well as commonest sights of the country is to see a boy or girl marching a number of cows, like so many soldiers, in double file and close rank from the pasture to the barn.

Niels, having been sent by his parents to thus bring a cow in from the field, the creature, though usually docile, suddenly became fractious and, running around the boy, tangled him up in the rope and then frantically dragged him through a grain field and against numerous obstructions before she could be stopped. When released the poor boy was found to have a broken thigh and other serious injuries, from the effects of which he was bedfast for more than three years. It was feared he never would recover, but his patient mother gave him the most devoted attention and relieved the tedium of his helplessness by teaching him needlework, at which she was adept, and by reading to him. In course of time he grew strong enough to be propped up in a chair and thus carried into the open air, but the exertion was probably too much for him, as he soon had a relapse, and during the ensuing two years spent most of his time in bed. His spine by degrees became so curved and deformed that, while his legs were nearly normal length, his body had the appearance of having been crumpled down thereon, and his large, well-shaped head crowded down between his shoulders.

In the year 1850 Apostle Erastus Snow arrived in Denmark as a missionary. He had not been there long when the gospel influence began to be felt and converts began to flock to his standard. One family among the residents of Lindholm embraced the gospel and soon found themselves somewhat notorious because of the attention they received from the local Lutheran priest, near whose chapel the family lived, and his frequent public comments on their abandonment of the Lutheran faith and acceptance of the unpopular doctrines of Mormonism.

In those days the Lutheran Church held almost undisputed sway throughout Denmark, and the invariable rule was for children to be diligently taught the Bible and drilled in a knowledge of the Lutheran creed from their infancy. When the children attain the age of about thirteen years, they are required to appear before the priest for a series of examinations as to their knowledge of these subjects before being confirmed as members of the Lutheran Church.

When Niels was fourteen years old, and was barely able to hobble about a little on crutches, he was cited to appear with a class of a dozen or more children before the priest, to be catechised. This they did many times until they were able to answer satisfactorily all the questions propounded to them. At about the first of these meetings a young girl asked to be excused from the examinations, because her parents had joined the Mormons, and she expected to. She cited in support of her plea, that the king of Denmark had granted religious liberty. Her request was complied with by the priest, who proceeded to comment on Mormonism then and at every subsequent meeting in a way that indicated that he must have been studying Mormon literature, and it was very strongly suspected that the priest was really converted to Mormonism, although he either lacked the courage to embrace it, or considered it impolitic to do so. Whether this surmise was correct or not, the priest seemed to have Mormonism constantly in his mind and his frequent allusions to its doctrines and the scripture supporting the same had the effect of converting Niels to Mormonism. Though he did not then declare his belief in the gospel, he had not from that time a doubt of its truth.

In the fall of 1856, when he was twenty years of age, Niels left home and went to live among relatives in Aalborg, where he had a checkered experience, often being made to feel that he was in the way and that his welcome was worn out, but occasionally encouraged by real kindness and genuine charity. One lady in particular took a great interest in him and, finding that he had some skill in needlework, encouraged him to practice a kind that was much in vogue among ladies, and through her kindly efforts he obtained considerable profitable work from many aristocratic women.

Soon after removing to Aalborg he met and became somewhat acquainted with some Mormons, a family of Saints being close neighbors to his aunt. His partial investigation of the gospel then confirmed his early conviction that it was the truth, but his dependent condition and the opposition of his relatives to such an unpopular religion led him to defer embracing it.

It was not until November 1, 1862, six years after he first attended a Mormon meeting, that he embraced the gospel and then under peculiar circumstances. Christoffer Jensen Kempe . . . was laboring as a Mormon missionary in that part of Denmark. One very stormy night he had found lodgings in a barn, about forty-two miles from Aalborg. Some time after retiring to rest he was aroused by feeling a hand laid upon his shoulder and hearing a voice tell him to get up and go to Aalborg and baptize the cripple, Larsen, whom he had seen at the Saints' meetings— that if he ever joined the Church he would have to be baptized the next evening. Obedient to the voice of the Spirit, he arose and

times been chided by his Lutheran acquaintances for doing so. Of course, Niels was not consulted in regard to the plans of the Lutheran ladies concerning him. His projected appointment was intended to be a surprise to him. The bishop announced to the ladies' society that he had complied with their petition and appointed Niels to act as lay preacher on the very day of the latter's baptism, as already mentioned, and that evening a meeting was held in the local Lutheran Church, and the announcement was made public. The inquiry was then made of the congregation as to where Niels lived, so that the news might be sent to him, but no person present seemed to know. One man, however, arose in the congregation and volunteered the information that he was acquainted with the brother of Niels (the same one whom Elder Kempe had hoped to baptize), and that he could carry the news to him of the honor that had come to Niels. He was accordingly commissioned to do so, but when he went to the brother the following day, he learned to his surprise that he was just one day too late; Niels had embraced Mormonism the night before. He knew it, for he had witnessed the baptism.

Niels learned, soon after he was confirmed a Latter-day Saint, of the proposition to make him a preacher of the Lutheran religion and, of course, was surprised thereat. He didn't regret having missed the opportunity, being sure (as he had been ever since he was a child) that Mormonism was true, he would have had to stultify himself to advocate any other creed. He was glad, however, that the temptation never was squarely presented to him, lest in his weakness and poverty he might have yielded to it.

George C. Lambert, *Treasures in Heaven* (Fifteenth book of the Faith-Promoting Series, Salt Lake City: Juvenile Instructor Office, 1914), pp. 7, 9-10, 13-17.

DEVIL DEFIES BAPTISM

George C. Lambert

During the night following his baptism, evil spirits seemed to fill the room in which Niels P. L. Eskildz had retired to sleep. They were not only terribly visible, but he heard voices also, taunting him with having acted foolishly in submitting to baptism and joining the Latter-day Saints.

He was told that he had deserted the only friends he ever had and would find no more among the Mormons, who would allow him to die of starvation rather than to assist him in his helpless, crippled condition, that he had no means of earning a livelihood in the far western land to which the Saints all hoped to migrate, and he would never cease to regret it if he ever went there.

This torment was kept up incessantly until he sought relief in prayer, and three times he got out of bed and tried to pray before he succeeded in doing so. Then his fervent pleading unto the Lord for power to withstand the temptation of the evil one, and to hold fast to the truth, brought relief to him. The evil spirits gradually, and with apparent reluctance, withdrew, and peace came to his soul, with the assurance that the Lord approved of his embracing the gospel, and that he could safely rely upon the Lord for future guidance.

> *Treasures in Heaven* (Fifteenth book of the Faith-Promoting Series, Salt Lake City: Juvenile Instructor Office, 1914), pp. 22-23.

A PERSONAGE IN WHITE STOOD BY YOUR SIDE

German E. Ellsworth

After my release as president of the Northern States Mission, Sister Ellsworth and I were invited to a dinner given by a railroad man and his wife by the name of DeWitt, who told us this story while dinner was being prepared:

He lived in the town of Valley Junction, Iowa, and the elders had visited his home many times. The local Methodist minister had warned, "If you don't quit entertaining those Mormon missionaries, you'll be led astray."

He assured the minister that his father and mother and grandparents had all been Methodists, and nothing would lead them astray, but he couldn't turn away these young men, for their songs entertained his children, and the spirit that they carried brought a heavenly influence into his home.

Two young missionaries came one time and said they were going to conference in Council Bluffs, and, since he was an engineer and it wouldn't cost him anything, why didn't he and his wife come to the conference and say goodbye to several elders who had been at their home and who were to be released?

He accepted the invitation after some hesitancy. When he arrived in Council Bluffs early in the morning, he found the address of the meeting place, which was an old store building next to a big grain and feed store, and was anything but imposing as a place to hold a conference.

He and his wife turned away disappointed, and walked several blocks. Finally he said, "We have come over two hundred miles to attend this conference and see those elders, and even though they are meeting in an old store building, I think we had better go back." So, they attended the meeting, sitting on opposite sides of the room, he with the elders, she with the sisters.

"During the service, several young missionaries were invited to speak, a song was sung, and then you stood and started to talk, and all of a sudden, a personage in white stood by your side and seemed to sanction all you said, and it went straight to my heart.

"When the meeting closed, I could hardly wait to get to my wife, and taking hold of her hand, I said, 'Mother, did anything happen to you in this meeting?'

"And she said, 'Yes. I saw someone in white standing by Elder Ellsworth all the time he talked, and I want to be baptized right now.'

"And that is why we applied for baptism following the first meeting we ever attended."

Autobiography of German E. Ellsworth, "This Christmas of 1953" (unpublished manuscript in the possession of Jaynann M. Payne, Provo, Utah), p. 17.

THE FIRST BAPTISM IN RUSSIA

The first baptism into the LDS Church in Russia occurred in April of 1895, under rather unusual circumstances that readily indicated that this event met with the approval of the Lord.

Mormon missionaries had been forbidden by law to enter upon Russian soil and preach their doctrines, which were not in harmony with the approved State Church of Russia. To do so was to be subject to arrest and rather harsh treatment. It was therefore quite surprising when Peter A. Sundwall, president of the Scandinavian Mission, received a letter from a gentleman residing in St. Petersburg, Russia, requesting that the elders be sent to Russia to perform the ordinance of baptism for him and his wife.[1]

The obligation to carry out their calling to preach the gospel and administer its ordinances to all of their Heavenly Father's children was foremost in the hearts and minds of these early Church missionaries. They would not, nor had they been, deterred by the possibility of imprisonment, physical harm and abuse at the hands of a civil authority, or an angry mob. Obedient to his calling, President Sundwall assigned Elder Agust Joel Hogland, president of the Goteberg Conference, to travel to St. Petersburg to honor this request to perform a sacred ordinance with the authority of the priesthood.

"President Hogland arrived in St. Petersburg Sunday evening, June 9, 1895, and was warmly welcomed by J. M. Lindelöf and his wife, who treated him to a splendid meal."[2] Immediately thereafter, a discussion ensued on the principles of the gospel, the three of them becoming so engrossed in discussing the restoration of these eternal truths that all desire for sleep left them, the conversation continuing until daybreak the following morning. Mr. Lindelöf again renewed his request for baptism, and it was agreed that the ordinance would be performed the following day.

"A boat was then hired and they rowed out on the Neva River, looking for a secluded spot to perform this sacred ordinance. The many people wading along the banks, some fishing and others sailing for pleasure, made it difficult to find the seclusion"[3] that they desired, and *had* to have.

---

[1]Mr. Lindelöf was a native of Finland, residing there until sixteen years prior to this event. It is possible that Brother Lindelöf's first contact with the Church, which brought him to investigate further and request baptism, could have come during this period of time.

[2]A. Dean Wengreen, *A History of the Church of Jesus Christ of Latter-day Saints in Sweden, 1850-1905* (Master's thesis, Brigham Young University, Provo, Utah), pp. 138-139.

[3]Ibid.

Finally a suitable place was located, but pleasure seekers abounded, depriving them of the privacy needed for safety. Elder Hogland records that he and his party then "united in prayer to God, pleading for his assistance and protection. In a short time, our prayer was heard, as both the boats and people began to leave the particular locality which we had selected. The ordinance was then performed and the new converts were confirmed members of the Church. Hands were laid on them for the reception of the Holy Ghost, after which we kneeled on the ground and thanked the Lord for his goodness, for we felt that the Lord had been with us."[4]

Elder Hogland then safely left the city of St. Petersburg on June 21, "after having ordained Brother Lindelöf an elder and instructing him in the duties of the priesthood."

---

[4]Andrew Jenson, *History of the Scandinavian Mission* (Salt Lake City: Deseret News Press, 1927), p. 343.

BLESSINGS

Every person will receive his just reward for the good he may do and for his every act. But let it be remembered that all blessings which we shall receive, either here or hereafter, must come to us as a result of our obedience to the laws of God upon which these blessings are predicated.

—Joseph F. Smith, *Improvement Era,*
16:71, November 1912

THE SPIRIT'S VOICE
Fenton L. Williams, Sr.

I have had many rich religious experiences in my life, but the single event that did the most to build my faith and make me want to shun all evil was an afternoon with a member of the Council of the Twelve who was visibly inspired to perform his duties. That man was Elder Harold B. Lee.

Our stake had just divided, and Elder Lee, then one of the Twelve, conducted a special Sunday afternoon meeting to set apart the high councilors, bishoprics, and other officers.

I knew these men well. I had worked for years with most of them as a member of the stake presidency, as a high councilor, and as stake Sunday School superintendent. I had visited in their homes. I had seen them perform various callings. I had been with them on outings and at parties and was familiar with their strengths and weaknesses.

However, our visiting apostle knew none of them personally. His contact with most of them amounted to little more than a handshake. Moreover, he was tired; he'd addressed both sessions of conference and was under the heavy strain of his great responsibilities.

As a member of the older stake presidency, I was invited to join in the laying on of hands as each of these men received his commission and blessing from the apostle. After the first two or three blessings, I found myself thinking, "He surely has read these men correctly—almost seems to know them."

As the blessings continued, I began listening intently to every word, tears welling in my eyes, as I began to realize that the pronouncements had not been by chance but by prophetic inspiration.

Here was a new bishop's counselor who would need to "always be on guard" to "honor his priesthood and calling." How well I knew it. Then followed one who had been having a tithing and coffee problem. His blessing contained specific warnings against those weaknesses. Next was a plodder type, level-headed, honest, and dependable, but not given much to reading. His blessing was a challenge to devote himself to scripture study, the one thing most needed by this fine man.

By this time, my tears flowed freely and I personally did some intense soul-searching about my worthiness to participate in that humbling hour. My hands tingled where they touched his on the heads of my brethren.

The blessings continued. A returned missionary, whose business often interfered with proper Sabbath observance, was told, "The Lord will bless and prosper you if you put his work first." Then followed a college professor who was a bit given to light-mindedness—an occasional vulgar story. "Your potentialities for good are limitless if you keep your thoughts and actions spotlessly clean."

I bear witness that not in one instance did that servant of the Lord fail to strike home. Several of the men who received blessings that day have since borne witness, in my hearing, of the prophetic utterances of our inspired visitor. They were from God.

Ensign, February 1974, pp. 27-28.

SAVED FROM DESTRUCTION
F. S. Wright

On the tenth of June, 1886, a volcanic eruption took place at Mount Tarawera, in New Zealand, which spread terror and destruction in the region round about. The event has been described as follows:

"A bright red glow became visible about the top of the mountain, the vivid flashes of light seemed to shoot up into the air. In an hour the flashes of light became what seemed a massive pillar of fire, rising, and increasing, and extending along the range. A dull rumbling accompanied it and became a terrific roar, with continuous explosions, loud thunder and vivid lightning, till heaven and earth seemed to be torn asunder. The air was filled with sulphurous odors, falling stones and mud. The village of Wairoa was annihilated, more than a hundred natives perished, and the fertile plains were covered with mud and ashes."

Mormon missionaries were laboring in New Zealand at the time, and the account of one of them, Elder F. S. Wright, of Coalville, Utah, tells of a most providential escape from destruction:

"After having spent about ten months in that locality and having become acquainted with the natives and their peculiar language, my missionary companion and I were desirous of visiting the Pink and White Terraces which nature had formed near the Rotomahana (a lake bordering on Mount Tarawera). Many tourists from all parts of the world used to visit the place on account of the beautiful scenery and to enjoy the healing virtues of the water. At a village called Wairoa, located on the shores of a beautiful lake, I had often received the kind hospitality of the natives, extended in their rude but hearty way.

"Wairoa is the terminus of the stage line, and from this point the tourists are conveyed in canoes across the lake, a distance of nine or ten miles, to the Terraces. The boat journey is made in the care of native guides, and the cost to each person is about twenty-five shillings. We had received a promise from the natives that they would take us across the lake when we desired to go. About 150 natives lived on the other side of the lake, and these we wanted to visit for the purpose of preaching to them.

"About the fifth of June, 1886, we again visited the natives of Wairoa, fully intending to cross the lake, to spend a few weeks among the natives in the hope of making some converts among them, and observe the beautiful Terraces which we had longed to see. But to our great surprise, when we arrived at Wairoa we found a feeling among the people manifested toward us different from any we had ever experienced before. At this particular time, there happened to be a Tangi, or feast, going on, the occasion being the death of one of their number, and many visitors were present.

"It was our observation, from having worked among these people, that they were more hospitable and receptive to our preaching when they were together in large numbers. We were therefore very much surprised at the strange reception which they gave us on this occasion. It was only through the influence of a few members of the Church, who were among the visitors at the feast, that we were granted the privilege of staying overnight. We had no opportunity to preach, nor were we allowed to conduct their morning and evening prayer services as we had done on other occasions.

"I am thoroughly convinced that it was a special interference of Providence that aroused that feeling among those natives which caused us to be directed away out of danger. On the following morning, we concluded that we could not succeed in completing our anticipated trip, so we journeyed back, stopping overnight at two places, and finally reaching Tepuke, our headquarters, twenty-four miles away from the place of the feast.

"We arrived there on the night of the ninth of June, and during the night the great catastrophe occurred, about 109 natives and 14 Europeans lost their lives, and mud from the eruption covered the country six to seven inches where we were. Complete darkness reigned until 11:00 A.M. the next day. Twenty-seven heavy shocks of earthquake were felt twelve or fourteen hours from the time it commenced. Shocks were felt daily for a number of weeks following. One result of this was that the cattle, sheep, and horses had to be driven out of that part of the country so that they could obtain food.

"A few days after the eruption we again journeyed back to the lake country on our way to the interior of the Island. We visited Wairoa, finding the Maori village, hotels and schoolhouse badly damaged. The erupted material at Wairoa was ten feet deep. Large trees had been knocked or blown down, and the roads through the brush or timbers were obstructed and travel was very difficult. An estimate of the dirt and rock thrown from Mount

Tarawera was made as one square half mile covered to the depth stated.

"I left home to perform my mission with a blessing pronounced upon me by a servant of God, that if I would go and perform an honorable mission to the best of my ability, I should be aided by the Spirit and power of God, and that I would return home in safety. I am here a living witness, and do testify to the world that these incidents did occur, and that I was guided by the kind hand of Providence to escape that dreadful calamity."

Stories of Courage and Devotion, 1926-1927
MIA manual for junior classes.

NONE SHALL STAY THEM
Edward James Wood

[A letter of February 12, 1916, from the First Presidency of the Church to Edward J. Wood asking him to serve a short-term mission to Samoa brought forth mixed feelings of joy and concern for Elder Wood. He rejoiced in being given the opportunity to again serve the Lord in this far-off land, but was much concerned as World War I was still very much under way, and he did not possess a passport. Travel between countries without a passport was not only forbidden, but impossible, as the immigration officers were most zealous and diligent in performing their duties.

The hand of the Lord was unmistakably evident in Elder Wood's trip to Samoa as he records:]

"I am a British subject by naturalization. I could not leave Canada without a passport, but the President of the Church had called me to be in Salt Lake City by an appointed time and asked if I could come. I should have obtained my passport before answering the letter, but I said, 'Yes, I will be there.' Then I set to work to make good my promise by applying through all the means available for my passport. The time approached for my departure, but the passport did not come. I presented the matter to the Lord in prayer and told him my difficulties. I felt that I must make good my word, and at least make the attempt to come, so I boarded the train bound for Salt Lake City without a passport.

"When I arrived at the boundary line, the emigration officers asked for my passport. The words, 'They shall go forth and none shall stay them' kept running through my mind. I thought of that, and wished that the emigration officer believed as much as I did of its truth, but he did not. However, I was somewhat acquainted with him, and he said, 'I will let you go, provided you furnish the passport later.'

" 'All right,' I agreed. 'I shall be pleased to do it.'

"When President Smith set me apart, he did not know anything about my not having a passport. I knew it would be more difficult to get out of the United States than to get in (leaving the port of San Francisco and getting to an American possession in Samoa). I knew, or thought I did, that I *must* have my passport. President Smith, laying his hands upon my head, said: 'Brother Wood, you shall go upon your mission to perform the business to be attended to, and return in safety.' All the time he was blessing me I was wondering about my passport.

"I was promised by our attorney that it should be registered to me in Salt Lake City and would be there the day after my arrival. I waited, and it did not come. I wired home to learn if any news had been received from Ottawa, the Washington of Canada. I did not get a reply. But President Smith said I should go— here was the prophecy and revelation that none should stay the disciples from preaching the gospel. The Lord had commanded me, not the emigration officers, so I set out on the train without my passport after receiving a wire at the station that my passport would be in San Francisco before the steamer left.

"I arrived in San Francisco and went down to the emigration office the day before the steamer sailed for I expected my passport would be there that evening, but it did not come. When the time came to answer the emigration officer, I got in line, knowing it would be all right, but I did not know how. The official began asking the passengers for passports, and some were refused, some were asked a lot of questions, but I stood there just as if I had a passport, and the official did not know anything different. When my time came, he said, 'Sit down a little while, Mr. Wood; I will talk to you later.'

"Well, I knew it would be all right. Did you ever feel that way, when you have just had the elders come in and administer to a sick child and you knew positively that the child would be healed? I felt these promises running through my mind, but how should they be fulfilled?

"When it came to my turn, the emigration officer said, 'Well, the time is up, you must come to the office tomorrow at nine as the steamer sails at one, Mr. Wood.'

"The time arrived, and I was in line even though I did not have a passport. I purposely stood in the rear of our company and heard the officer in charge calling for passports in no uncertain terms. Again the promise, 'They shall go forth and none shall stay them' ran through my mind, when all at once, to the surprise of the passengers, the officer called out, 'Is Mr. Wood close by?'

"I said, 'Yes, sir.'

"He answered, 'Please come right up here!'

"I wondered what he would do with me without any passport, when to my great surprise, he said, 'Mr. Wood, you have been twice before to the Islands?'

" 'Yes, sir.'

" 'All right,' he said, 'we have a very large passenger list here, and to save time, please come up here and receive the passports to help us out.'

"He never asked for mine at all. I went and stood by his side and asked those of our company and many others for their passports. No one may ever know how my heart rejoiced at this turn of affairs.

"After all were on board the steamer, the officer thanked me for helping, and said that the captain would like to have a talk with me in the morning about the mission work we were doing on the Islands. Then, the emigration officer said, 'Let's see, Mr. Wood, you have your passport, go right on board the steamer.'

"I did not have a passport, though I had the commission from President Smith, which was worth more than all the passports from all the governments in the world.

"The next morning, passengers were lined up on the deck and the doctor and the purser examined everyone for health and to see that all had the necessary credentials, passports, etc. Again I wondered just how to get by when the purser came to me and asked me to sit down, saying, 'Of course, you understand you must present your passport, Mr. Wood.'

" 'All right,' I said. 'I understand it.'

" 'Where did you come from?'

" 'From Canada.'

" 'I am delighted to see you people from Canada so willing to go and preach the gospel to those natives.'

"And I spoke of the gospel with him, and he asked for no passport at all.

"Then the captain sent for me to go to his office and talk with him about our mission. I did this while the other passengers were being examined. The captain never mentioned my passport, but was very interested in talking about what our Church was doing among the natives of the different islands.

"After five days of nice weather, we were in Honolulu harbor in the Hawaiian Islands. Several of our group were to labor there, and all other passengers were allowed to go ashore for several hours, but once more our passports had to be shown. I lined up with the others and again wondered how I would get along, as no one among the officers knew I didn't have a passport, but again the promise ran through my mind. Then, to the surprise of many, a native stood on the wharf and said to me, 'Aloha nui.'

"The officer who was examining the passengers' passports turned to me and said, 'Are you acquainted with that native? He seems to know you, and wants to see you.'

" 'Yes,' I said, 'I would like to hurry ashore and have a little visit with him.'

" 'All right, go right ahead. We will stay here about six or seven hours.'

"Once more the hand of Providence was with me, but now I was in a more difficult position than before. In five or six days I would be in Samoa and there were only a few others that would be getting off there and we would all have to show our passports. What would happen if the officers found out I had come all this way without a passport?"

[A few days later the ship entered Pago Pago harbor at Tutuila, American Samoa, where a large group of Latter-day Saints gathered at the wharf to meet Elder Wood.]

"There were only a few strangers besides our company and myself to get off," Elder Wood continued, "and, as usual, I purposely put myself the last one, asking the Lord to again come to my rescue! The natives and elders were calling to me and greeting me, saying how pleased they were to see me.

"Then the emigration officer said, 'Sit down, Mr. Wood, I want to ask you a question. Get your passport ready.'

" 'All right.'

"It was my turn to present my passport when he turned to the man next to me and said, 'Why, you are a New Yorker.'

"The officer then went over and had a conversation with the man he had called the 'New Yorker,' and when he came back, he said, 'Let me see, Mr. Wood, I have had your passport all right, you may go on. As these people on shore are anxious to have you go ashore we will allow you to go at once, and we wish you every success on your visit. We have enjoyed the several talks we have had during the voyage from San Francisco. I will be pleased if you return on our ship.'

" 'I appreciate your kindness to me while on the journey, and will certainly be glad to be again in your company when I have finished my mission here in Samoa,' I replied.

"I shook hands with them and went down the gangplank and shook hands with the crowd of Samoans and elders. Many of the natives I had baptized years before while there on my other two missions. The native Saints, and of course the missionaries, gave me a real welcome.

"I attended to the business I was called to attend to for the Church, and I can never forget how the Lord, through his Spirit, intervened by impressing all the officers to assist me without ever asking for my papers."

Melvin S. Tagg, *The Life of Edward James Wood—Church Patriot* (Master's thesis, Brigham Young University, Provo, Utah, July 1959), pp. 97-101. Edited by compiler.

THE CONSTANT PROTECTOR

In the late 1800s, young elders went forth on their missions with faith not only in the doctrines that they were called upon to preach, but also faith in the Lord and his promise of protection for his servants as they delivered their generally unwelcome message of repentance and restoration of the everlasting gospel. More often than not, rejection and open hostility was manifested towards them, and it was not uncommon for these early missionaries of the Church to have their very lives threatened for merely having let it be known that they were members of the Mormon Church.

Shortly after arriving in Samoa in 1839, Elder Edward J. Wood soon found that many of the natives would have found greater joy in physically abusing him than in listening to his message of restored truths. But Elder Wood proved himself to be a true servant of the Lord and continued to faithfully discharge his duties in spite of the opposition he encountered. More than once he gratefully acknowledged the hand of the Lord in preserving his life, and after one such occasion he recorded:

"I was traveling among the natives on one of the largest islands of the group. I was living in a large village with a good man and his wife who had joined the Church on another island. The native ministers—"teachers" as they were called by the natives— were very bitter towards me and did all they could to get me to leave the island. However, the couple I was staying with were very kind. While the village was getting ready to visit another island, this couple asked me to go along with them in their large native-made boat, as the village they were to visit was the home of her parents. All the villages of any size are near the coast, and the natives always travel from one village to another by boat or native canoe. I was glad to accept the invitation, although I learned on the boat that I was a very unwelcome member of the company of seventy-five people.

"We had scarcely left the little bay and were getting out to sea when a terrible storm came up. It was a real typhoon—it soon blew so hard we could not return and expected to be swamped with every white-capped wave. The natives decided that it was all brought about by having a *Mamona*—a Mormon missionary —aboard. They called me Jonah, and decided to throw me overboard. The whole boat load seemed conspired against me, except our brother and his good wife."[1]

One rough, strong, and evil-designing native then approached Elder Wood with the intent of throwing him overboard. Grossly outnumbered and slight of build and therefore not a suitable match

---

[1]Melvin S. Tagg, *The Life of Edward James Wood—Church Patriot* (Master's thesis, Brigham Young University, Provo, Utah, July 1959), pp. 38-39.

for the big, burly native, it appeared that Elder Wood's days as a missionary in this estate were coming to a very sad and abrupt end in a matter of moments.

Just as the big native was about to take him in his grasp and cast him to his fate with the sharks, Elder Wood challenged, "You wouldn't really throw me overboard, would you?"

"Well, I was going to," replied the superstitious native, "but I don't *feel* like it now," and he returned to his seat.

The winds and the waves calmed and the boat continued safely on to its destination where it docked with all seventy-five passengers on board, including the *Mamona*.

It was then that Elder Wood remembered a promise given him by George Q. Cannon when he was set apart for his mission in which the Holy Spirit was promised as a constant protector, comforter, and guide; and the hearts of evil-designing men who would seek to do him harm would be softened when they came under the influence of the Holy Spirit around him.

ELEMENTS SUBJECT TO MISSIONARY'S CONTROL

[Early in 1896, the First Presidency of the Church called Edward Wood to return to Samoa as mission president. Prior to his departure he was given a missionary blessing by Seymour B. Young in which President Wood was promised that "the elements will be subject to your control. They shall neither destroy you nor retard your travel on land or sea." For one who knew the dangers of traveling about the Samoan Mission, this blessing must have been of great comfort to him then, and even more so on April 7, 1896, when President Wood recorded:]

"We had a mission conference appointed at our headquarters. I was visiting on Savaii, our largest island, and with a number of natives planned to leave this island and cross the channel between the two islands, about fifteen miles distant. While we were holding a meeting, a strong wind arose, making a very rough sea covered with whitecaps and very heavy swells, and making it extremely dangerous for small boats such as we had for the crossing. What a disappointment it would be for those at the conference if we did not arrive at the meeting."

[It was then that one of the natives suggested that the group repair to the sandy beach to hold an open-air prayer service. The native then requested that President Wood offer a prayer and rebuke the wind and waves so that they could cross the channel in safety. The group then sang a hymn of praise to the Lord and knelt on the beach as President Wood asked the Lord to calm enough of the surface of the ocean so that their boats might cross over the channel in safety.]

"After that prayer," Elder Wood continued, "we bade goodbye to those who were remaining on the island and launched our boats and were soon out of the lagoon in mid-ocean. To our great surprise and gratitude, a smooth lane lay before us all the way across. It was about one hundred feet wide, while on either side the waves were mountainous and the wind very strong. As soon as we set foot on the beach of the other island, we again knelt in prayer and thanked God for preserving our lives and for calming the ocean.

"During the conference most of the native Saints in our company bore testimony to our deliverance through the goodness of God in calming the waves for our crossing. Surely it was a time of general rejoicing, for the promise given two years earlier in a missionary blessing had been marvelously fulfilled."

Melvin S. Tagg, *The Life of Edward James Wood—Church Patriot* (Master's thesis, Brigham Young University, Provo, Utah, 1959), pp. 43-44; 50-51. Edited by compiler.

BOOK OF MORMON

We are called a peculiar people because, perchance, we thoroughly believe and obey the gospel of Jesus Christ. Our peculiarity lies very largely in the fact that we believe the Old and New Testaments actually contain the word of the Lord, as far as translated correctly. We also firmly believe the Book of Mormon, which the world knows comparatively little of; and add to that unwavering belief in the Doctrine and Covenants and Pearl of Great Price. We regard the teachings contained therein as revelations of our Father in heaven to his children who dwell upon this earth.

—George Albert Smith, *Conference Report,*
October 1905, p. 26

THE LORD FINDS A SCRIPTURE
Gregory G. Vernon

Every missionary has the experience of knocking on that one last door before he retires for the evening and there being met with success. In one particular part of the city of Anchorage where we were laboring, we had met with good success during the day and had introduced ourselves, given discussions, and left copies of the Book of Mormon with several people. We had had unusual success; in fact, we were congratulating ourselves on a day well spent and a job well done as we proceeded to turn homeward. Our conversation was to the effect that we were pleased with the good day's work and had made some significant contacts with people who seemed to be genuinely interested in our message.

Nevertheless, as we turned down a street, we were impressed to stop at the last home on that street, which we did. We were met by a fine-looking, fair-haired young mother with children at her side, who invited us in. We gave them a discussion and made an appointment to come back the following evening, which we did.

The discussion the second night was not going well and we felt a sense of frustration and a certain inability to impress upon this family the spiritual nature of our message. Finally, as we were about to leave, I recalled what some other missionaries in our mission had told me that they had done when they just didn't seem to be getting anywhere during a discussion with a prospective family. That was to take their copy of the Book of Mormon and let it fall open to a page at random, trusting in the guidance of the Lord that that particular scripture would impress upon the investigator some point or element of the gospel that would be particularly relevant to his own needs and thoughts. I determined to try this tack, and, without really possessing much faith that it would work, opened my copy of the Book of Mormon at random and commenced to read those few verses that seemed to impress me.

The verses that I turned to contained one of the only references in the Book of Mormon to a man by the name of Hagoth, who was a ship builder. The reference to him indicates only that he built a ship which he loaded with people and sailed away to the north country; he returned some time later and took another ship load of people to the north country, and was never heard of again. (Alma 63:5-9.)

After reading that scripture to this family, I felt that I certainly had turned to the wrong page, and had not come up with any kind of scripture that could possibly influence them in any manner. I suppose I had my mind set on reading some profound discourse of King Benjamin or Moroni on baptism, or a scripture on the appearance of Christ to the American people, or some other seemingly profound or interesting documentation from the Book of Mormon. Instead, I had turned to and read a brief and sketchy account of one of the very minor figures in the Book of Mormon. I thought that my efforts had certainly been in vain, and that even though the technique had worked for other missionaries, it certainly had not worked for me!

I was preparing to make an apology for reading a scripture that was so out of place and had nothing at all to do with the discussion of the evening, when I noticed a look of intense concentration on the faces of this young couple. They turned to each other and, with a startled look, asked me to *repeat* the scripture that I had just read.

After I had done so, the wife told me that they were Haida Indians and that their people resided in the Queen Charlotte Islands and points further north into Alaska. Their countenance was fair and they were fair-skinned people, not possessing those physical traits which are normally associated with the Lamanite people.

She proceeded to tell me that her great-grandfather, who had been one of the leaders of the Haida Nation, had, when she was a very small girl, told her the story of the origin of her people and that story closely paralleled this brief reference to Hagoth in the Book of Mormon! She indicated to me that the name Hagoth was a name with which she was acquainted in the annals of tribal history and a responsive cord had been struck when I read that scripture.

Shortly thereafter I was called to a position of leadership in the mission and left the area. However, this fine family was subsequently brought into the Church and I was told had developed an insatiable appetite for the Book of Mormon.

THE MORNING AFTER
Barbara Gail Mikeska

There is a popular song with special meaning to me. It says, "There's got to be a morning after." I would like to share with you my "morning after."

My conversion to The Church of Jesus Christ of Latter-day Saints was through the Book of Mormon, but it is not the usual "missionary meets potential investigator" story.

I was the first born in a Catholic family of five children. At an early age I can remember us as a family kneeling together for evening prayer and reciting of the rosary. Even though as children we balked at this practice and it didn't last long, we were instilled with a deep feeling of love for Jesus and God. My parents diligently sent us to catechism classes and saw to it that we attended Mass on Sunday. I will always be grateful for having had loving parents and for having been reared in a Christian home.

As the years passed and I grew up, I developed into a rather serious-minded girl and a deep longing to serve the Lord became my secret desire. As do many "good" Catholic girls at sometime or other, in my senior year of high school I began to give consideration to joining a convent. And yet, an equally strong desire to marry, have children, *and* serve the Lord seemed to confuse the issue. Finally, after presenting my problem to the Lord in prayer, the desire to be a nun left me entirely. It was one of the most remarkable answers to a prayer that I had yet received.

Well, I grew into womanhood and became a career girl with both eyes and all my heart looking out for "Mr. Right." To make a long story short, I never found him. Instead, I found that when someone said, "I love you," they didn't always mean it.

Years went by, in which I had survived several romances, major back surgery, and numerous family crises. My life began to be filled with many personal problems and I was taking a course away from God, all of which began to weigh heavily upon my heart. Once again, as I had done many times, I hopefully took my problems to the Lord. I wanted and needed his help, his guidance, his forgiveness. I had questions with no answers. Many times when I was in a reflective state of mind, I would drive to the Catholic church at night when I knew no one would be there, I would go in and, kneeling down at the altar, I would pray to the Lord with all my heart for his blessing. Often I would simply kneel for great lengths of time, waiting to feel his presence. Always— nothing.

I can recall times when I was yet a teenager that I would take a walk by myself at night and carry on a long conversation with God. At those times, for some reason I didn't then understand, I felt extremely close to my God, as though at some time I had once been in his presence; as though he knew me and I knew him, personally. I never told anyone that because I knew they would think me presumptuous.

In my then state of confusion I began to search for the "feeling" or the presence of the Lord that I wanted and needed so much. I began looking into and then attending services at the Jewish and Baptist churches. Then, in the office where I worked there came a new man who soon became known to everyone as a Mormon, a really "peculiar" person.

Gradually we became friends and occasionally he would make reference to a certain aspect of his religion. I remember asking him one day out of curiosity if I might read what he called the Book of Mormon, having no idea what it was other than that it contained doctrines of his faith. I also remember his saying that he didn't feel I was serious about it or ready for it. The conversation was soon forgotten.

Months went by and I began to witness a change in both my friend and myself. He became less loyal to the teachings he professed and I became genuinely interested. Significantly, at this time my way of life and lack of spiritual fulfillment became more than I could handle alone. For several weeks I had taken to pleading with the Lord for a means to change the direction of my life so that I would be able to attain for myself all the things that I had held dear; namely, a close relationship with him, a family of my own, and a church in which he dwelled.

One evening when I was engaged in such pleading with the Lord, an overwhelming feeling of despair engulfed me. I felt as though I didn't want to, nor could, live any longer in this world without knowing God and his desires for me. In my praying I soon became distraught to the point of self-destruction. I began to weep as I rose from my knees and slowly walked to the medicine chest in the bathroom of my apartment. The first thing I reached for were razor blades for slitting my wrists, but I couldn't bring myself to do this. Then I looked at my face in the bathroom mirror. The image I saw was blurred through the tears that were streaming down my face. Still looking at my image in the mirror, and reaching for every bottle of pills I could get my hands on, I pleaded with my Lord as I began to swallow hands full of pills, "My God, my God, you know I don't want to do this! Where in the world *are* you?"

Almost immediately I realized the seriousness of what I had just done, and attempted to call my brother who lived in the same apartment complex. I simply cried into the phone and as my eyes closed a feeling came over me that made me think, "Don't worry, everything will be all right. From now on, your life will be entirely different."

The next thing I felt was the terrible discomfort of having my stomach pumped. I was in the hospital for only one night and then I returned home to my apartment, much to the concern of my beloved family. But I felt I must return to my own home to thank the Lord for sparing my life and to await his instruction, which I felt sure was to come.

Later that same morning my Mormon friend came to see me, saying, "I've brought you a book to read. I think you need it now." Suddenly a feeling filled my heart nearly to bursting and I thought to myself, "Oh, please, let it be the Book of Mormon," not really knowing what the Book of Mormon was. I could hardly wait for my visitor to leave, I was filled with such excitement.

When I was alone again, I carefully carried the book into the bedroom with me and got into bed. For what seemed an eternity I sat looking down at the book I held in my hands. Quietly I began to weep and to tremble with joy. I knew that whatever was contained within the pages of this book, the very receiving of this book was the answer to my life-and-death plea to my Father in heaven. There was a presence in my room at that moment that warmed me from head to toe and assured me that all was well and right, and I knew in that same moment that I would soon be committed to what I was about to read. And, yes, I knew that this was where God would be, that this was God's truth. I was not disappointed in my reading.

A couple of weeks later I invited myself to Church and after services asked to be taught by two of the loveliest lady missionaries you would ever want to meet.

Eternally grateful to my Heavenly Father, with a feeling I will never fully be able to express, I was baptized a member of the Church of Jesus Christ on November 27, 1971, ten days before my twenty-fourth birthday.

I want my sweet family to know that I am certain that this is the will of the Lord, that The Church of Jesus Christ of Latter-day Saints is indeed his restored Church, and that I love them dearly and am thankful for them.

I give this testimony in the name of Jesus Christ.

VOICES FROM THE BOOK OF MORMON
Elder Rex D. Pinegar

One young husband decided to find out for himself if the Church was true. He had observed the uplifting changes brought into the lives of his wife and children, who had joined The Church of Jesus Christ of Latter-day Saints six years previously. He obtained a copy of the Book of Mormon and began reading. At first he felt nothing, but he continued to read. He remembered that he should pray as he read—that was the counsel the missionaries had given. For the next six evenings he continued to read and to pray. He continued to plead with the Lord to let him know the truths contained in these scriptures.

Two more evenings he continued, and then a deeply spiritual experience began to unfold. He found himself listening as he read. It was as though he were hearing the characters in the story speak rather than verbalizing the printed word himself. He continued to pray and to study. At the close of the tenth evening, he stated that he was now *hearing the voices* of the characters and feeling the spirit of their messages.

His continued effort brought him near to the Lord in his search for truth; he then received a testimony of the truthfulness of the Book of Mormon.

From an address delivered at the 144th Semiannual General Conference, October 5, 1974.

I DON'T BELIEVE THE STORY!

Jonathon Calkins Wright was determined to make something of his life, so he studied and prepared to be a Methodist minister. Not too long after realizing this ambition, his brother-in-law, Lyman L. Corry, asked for the privilege of preaching in the little church over which Jonathon presided. Corry was uneducated and unqualified in the language of the ministry, but that did not prevent him from officiating as a Mormon preacher, which was rather disconcerting to a man of Jonathon's position. Jonathon was rather slow to grant his brother-in-law's request, but he was sufficiently broad-minded that he finally consented, even agreeing to attend and listen to the sermon to be preached by the Mormon missionary.

Corry began his meeting by singing a hymn, after which the members of the congregation were quick to agree that although this new "preacher" was not lacking in dedication to his cause, he was definitely wanting in musical ability. But when he commenced to pray to his Father in heaven, Jonathon's impression began to change. Corry then began to preach, and so powerful was his message that within fifteen minutes, Jonathon relates, "my props were knocked clear from under me. I had no foundation left, none whatever, to stand on."[1]

Following the meeting, Corry offered Jonathon a Book of Mormon, which he accepted and began to read just as soon as his brother-in-law departed. Bedtime came, but still he read on, until he felt compelled to know for a certainty the truthfulness of the book of modern-day scriptures that he was reading, stating to his wife, "Rebecca, I *must* see this man Joseph Smith!"

"I wish you would," she replied. "You'll never have any peace until you do!"

As soon as he could manage his affairs, Jonathon mounted his horse and started for Nauvoo, which was some eighty miles away, stopping only when necessary to rest and feed the horse. Then, while his horse was grazing, Jonathon would sit beneath the nearest inviting shady tree and read the Book of Mormon. He had not read far when he read something that put a check on his interest, and shutting the book with a bang, he said to himself, "I'll not go another step! I'm going right back home. I don't believe the story!"

His horse was standing nearby and as he approached the animal it started for him, eyes wildly bulging, its mouth wide open in a most vicious manner, and behaving generally as if it had suddenly gone mad. Jonathon's attempts to mount his horse for the return journey were met with resistance as the animal whirled and kicked at him. The horse seemed determined to fight every effort on Jonathon's part to subdue him. It then broke loose and ran wildly from him, leaving Jonathon afoot.

[1]Brigham Wright, "A Sketch of the Life of Jonathan Calkins Wright" (unpublished manuscript in the possession of his granddaughter, Ruth Pearse Wallace, Woodland Hills, California).

Jonathon started after his horse, and within a short time came upon some men who inquired if he was the one who owned the horse that had been running loose. "He sure is full of the devil," they said. "We finally caught him and tied him in a corner of the fence in the lane, but he is in an awful condition!"

Jonathon thanked the men for their assistance and hurried on to where he had been directed. As he approached his horse, that ordinarily was as gentle an animal as one would wish to own, it again came towards him—as close as the rope restraining it would permit—manifesting the same vicious behavior as before.

"Right then and there," Jonathon states, "I promised the Lord that I would go and see Joseph Smith, if He would take the devil out of my horse."

As soon as he had made that promise, the horse dropped his head and opened its mouth to receive the bit and bridle, as gently as it had always done before. Jonathon then mounted his horse and continued on his way to keep his commitment to the Lord.

Upon arriving in Nauvoo, he inquired after the Prophet Joseph Smith from a man who was driving his cows into his yard. "Joseph Smith is not here," the man replied. "I am his brother, Hyrum Smith. Is there anything I can do for you?"

Hyrum offered his hospitality, suggesting that Jonathon stay the night so that they might talk over the matter of religion. After an evening meal, they began to discuss this new religion and the scriptures that had come forth, continuing in their conversation until the break of day. Jonathon was convinced of the truthfulness of the gospel and the divinity of the Book of Mormon and early that morning accompanied Hyrum Smith to the Mississippi River where he was baptized and confirmed a member of the Church.

Jonathon finally met Joseph Smith, but only after the Prophet and his brother, Hyrum, were brought back to Nauvoo after their martyrdom. He continued thereafter in many faithful years of service to the Church, always acknowledging the hand of the Lord in preventing him from rejecting the Book of Mormon and returning home without seeking out the testimony of Joseph and Hyrum by allowing his horse to be afflicted by the evil one.

FINDING THE WORD OF GOD

Gregg Weaver

In May of 1968, amid riots and wars and an uncertain future, I found my life was void of any meaning. I searched intensely the religious philosophies of the world to find inner peace, direction, and the stuff that makes life worthwhile. It was only after experiencing failure and despair that, as a last resort, I turned my thoughts toward God, our Father, and completely dedicated my life to serving and obeying him. I was filled with the love of God, and had direction in my life. Yet, as I dealt with the difficulties and perplexities of life, I soon discovered that something was missing, but I didn't know exactly what. I needed something more to guide me, to enlighten my mind, and to define what was right.

Then, while walking to class one day, the thought came to me that many people the world over believed that there was one who came to earth as the Son of God. If that were really so, his words would further enlighten me concerning God and could be of great worth to me. I had investigated many religious philosophies, but had totally ignored Christianity. I had been discouraged with Christianity as a way of life, as my observations had been that Christians generally did not live the precepts of their religion.

I had never read the Bible, but I knew the book was about Him. The possibility of finally gaining a knowledge of the plan of life and God's desires for his children here on earth so possessed me that I determined to read the Bible—now. I didn't go to that next class; I went home. I *had* to find out about the Son of God.

I decided that I was going to take the Bible and walk up into the mountains near my home where I could have undisturbed peace and read, and I was not coming back until I had the answers I had to have. I walked into the house and went directly to the bookcase. On the lower shelf was a Bible, next to it a Book of Mormon and a Doctrine and Covenants. I had every intention of taking the Bible and reading about the Son of God, and yet, as I reached forth to grasp the Bible, my hand went to the Book of Mormon. As I was making my way to the door, I suddenly realized that I had the Book of Mormon in my hand. "I don't want this book," I told myself. "I want the Bible, and it's still on the bookshelf. What am I doing with the Book of Mormon? I want to know about Christ!"

I went back to the bookshelf, determined to get the Bible this time. As I reached out to put my hand on the Bible, it was as if my hand was operating totally independent of my thoughts and actions. This time I retrieved the Doctrine and Covenants. This really threw me!

While standing there puzzling over those two books I had in my hands, books towards which I had only feelings of rejection and antagonism, and that I had no desire whatsoever to read, I found myself being ushered out the door and I was on my way to City Creek Canyon. My legs were fast putting distance between me and the house, an action my mind was fighting. I wanted to go back to that bookshelf and get the Bible, but I was powerless to do so. As I began to recognize the futility of carrying out my desires, and my seemingly helpless condition, I decided to accept the situation as it existed and ceased resisting. I immediately began to feel peaceful, happy, and contented, and experienced the most pleasant walk of my life.

I began climbing the mountain, anxious to find a secluded spot to read the books I held in my hands. Finding such a place, I sat down and opened the Book of Mormon. Inside was an inscription: "To Gregg, For interest and participation in Sunday School." At first, I couldn't recall ever attending Sunday School, then I vaguely began to remember attending a class in which the Sunday School teacher had presented everyone with a Book of Mormon.

I read the Joseph Smith story, the testimony of the witnesses, and then began to read, "I, Nephi, having been born of goodly parents. . . ." I had not read far when an intensely warm feeling came over me and I felt as if I were glowing from within. My soul was filled to overflowing; as though in a moment I would no longer be able to contain this beautiful feeling within me.

Tears trickled off my cheeks as I continued to read and be filled by the Spirit. I knew that that which I was reading was true; that this book had to have been written by prophets, men of God. I had found what I was looking for—the word of God— in the Book of Mormon! My very soul burned with this testimony as the Spirit enclosed me in the most beautiful, warm, wonderful way. The Spirit continued with me as I read through that day and on into the night, until there was not light enough to see the sacred words. My heart was full as I walked home that night, so very grateful to the Lord for the knowledge he had given me.

It is now my concern that I will always live my life so as to be worthy to continue raising my voice in testimony as to the truthfulness of the Book of Mormon and the restoration of the gospel—a very small price to pay for the beautiful testimony I received of the divinity of the Book of Mormon.

CHRIST

He that hath my commandments, and keepeth them, he it is that loveth me: and he that loveth me shall be loved of my Father, and I will love him, and will manifest myself to him.

—John 14:21

THE SAVIOR HAS BEEN IN YOUR MIDST
Mary Elizabeth Rollins Lightner

A few evenings after [Joseph Smith's] visit to our house, Mother and I went over to the Smith house. There were other visitors. The whole Smith family, excepting Joseph, was there. As we stood talking to them, Brother Joseph and Martin Harris came in, with two or three others. When the greetings were over, Brother Joseph looked around very solemnly. It was the first time some of them had ever seen him. He then said, "There are enough here to hold a little meeting."

A board was put across two chairs to make seats. Martin Harris sat on a little box at Joseph's feet. They sang and prayed; then Joseph got up to speak. He began very solemnly and very earnestly. All at once his countenance changed and he stood mute. He turned so white he seemed perfectly transparent. Those who looked at him that night said he looked like he had a searchlight within him, in every part of his body. I never saw anything like it on earth. I could not take my eyes away from him. He got so white that anyone who saw him would have thought he was transparent. I remember I thought we could almost see the bones through the flesh of his face. I shall remember it and see it in my mind's eye as long as I remain upon the earth.

He stood some moments looking over the congregation, as if to pierce each heart, then said, "Do you know who has been in your midst this night?"

One of the Smiths said, "An angel of the Lord."

Joseph did not answer. Martin Harris was sitting at the Prophet's feet on a box. He slid to his knees, clasped his arms around the Prophet's knees and said, "I know; it was our Lord and Savior, Jesus Christ."

Joseph put his hand on Martin's head and answered, "Martin, God revealed that to you. Brothers and Sisters, the Savior has been in your midst this night. I want you all to remember it. There is a veil over your eyes, for you could not endure to look upon him. You must be fed with milk and not strong meat. I want you to remember this as if it were the last thing that escaped my lips. He has given you all to me, and commanded me to seal you up to everlasting life, that where he is there you may be also. And if you are tempted of Satan say, 'Get thee behind me, Satan, for my salvation is secure.' "

Then he knelt and prayed, and such a prayer I never heard before or since. I felt he was talking to the Lord, and the power rested upon us all.

Diary of Mary Elizabeth Rollins Lightner, *Young Woman's Journal*, XVI, Dec. 1905, pp. 556-557.

I KNOW THAT THE LORD LIVES!
Elder Melvin J. Ballard

I bear witness to you that I know that the Lord lives. I know that he has made this sacrifice and this atonement. He has given me a foretaste of these things.

I recall an experience which I had two years ago—bearing witness to my soul of the reality of his death, of his crucifixion, and his resurrection—that I shall never forget. I bear it to you tonight, to you, young boys and girls; not with a spirit to glory over it, but with a grateful heart and with thanksgiving in my soul. I know that he lives, and I know that through him men must find their salvation, and that we cannot ignore this blessed offering that he has given us as the means of our spiritual growth to prepare us to come to him and be justified.

Away on the Fort Peck Reservation where I was doing missionary work with some of the brethren, laboring among the Indians, seeking the Lord for light to decide certain matters pertaining to our work there, and receiving a witness from him that we were doing things according to his will, I found myself one evening in the dreams of the night in that sacred building, the temple. After a season of prayer and rejoicing I was informed that I should have the privilege of entering into one of those rooms to meet a glorious Personage, and, as I entered the door, I saw, seated on a raised platform, the most glorious Being my eyes have ever beheld or that I ever conceived existed in all the eternal worlds. As I approached to be introduced, he arose and stepped towards me with extended arms, and he smiled as he softly spoke my name. If I shall live to be a million years old, I shall never forget that smile. He took me into his arms and kissed me, pressed me to his bosom, and blessed me, until the marrow of my bones seemed to melt! When he had finished, I fell at his feet and, as I bathed them with my tears and kisses, I saw the prints of the nails in the feet of the Redeemer of the world. The feeling that I had in the presence of him who hath all things in his hands, to have his love, his affection, and his blessing was such that if I ever can receive that of which I had but a foretaste, I would give all that I am, all that I ever hope to be, to feel what I then felt!

> From an address delivered at the Mutual Improvement Association Conference, June 1916.

THE SAVIOR STOOD HERE!

Leroi C. Snow

For some time President Woodruff's health had been failing. Nearly every evening President Lorenzo Snow visited him at his home on South Fifth East Street. This particular evening the doctors said President Woodruff was failing rapidly, and they feared he would not live much longer. Lorenzo Snow was then president of the Council of Twelve and was greatly worried over the possibility of succeeding President Woodruff, especially because of the terrible financial condition of the Church. Referring to this condition, President Heber J. Grant has said: "The Church was in a financial slough of despond, so to speak, almost financially bankrupt—its credit was hardly good for a thousand dollars without security."

My father went to his room in the Salt Lake Temple, where he was residing at the time. He dressed in his robes of the priesthood, went into the Holy of Holies, there in the house of the Lord, and knelt at the sacred altar. He pleaded with the Lord to spare President Woodruff's life, that President Woodruff might outlive him and that the great responsibility of Church leadership would never fall upon his shoulders. Yet he promised the Lord that he would devotedly perform any duty required at his hands. At this time he was in his eighty-fourth year. Soon after this President Woodruff was taken to California, where he died Friday morning at 6:40 o'clock, September 2, 1898. President George Q. Cannon at once wired the sad information to the President's office in Salt Lake City. Word was forwarded to President Snow, who was in Brigham City. The telegram was delivered to him on the streets of Brigham. He read it to Rudger Clawson, then president of Box Elder Stake, who was with him, went to the telegraph office and replied that he would leave on the train about 5:30 that evening. He reached Salt Lake City about 7:15, proceeded to the president's oval office, gave some instructions and then went to his private room in the Salt Lake Temple.

President Snow put on his holy temple robes, repaired again to the same sacred altar, offered up the signs of the priesthood; and poured out his heart to the Lord. He reminded the Lord how he had pleaded for President Woodruff's life and that his days might be lengthened beyond his own; that he might never be called upon to bear the heavy burdens and responsibilities of Church leadership. "Nevertheless," he said, "thy will be done. I have not sought this responsibility, but if it be thy will, I now present myself before thee for thy guidance and instruction. I ask that thou show me what thou wouldst have me do."

After finishing his prayer, he expected a reply, some special manifestation from the Lord. So he waited—and waited—and waited. There was no reply, no voice, no visitation, no manifestation. He left the altar and the room in great disappointment. He passed through the celestial room and out into the large corridor leading to his own room, where a most glorious manifestation was given President Snow. One of the most beautiful accounts of this experience is told by his granddaughter, Allie Young Pond:

"One evening when I was visiting Grandpa Snow in his room in the Salt Lake Temple, I remained until the doorkeepers had gone and the night watchman had not yet come in, so Grandpa said he would take me to the main front entrance and let me out that way. He got his bunch of keys from his dresser. After we left his room and while we were still in the large corridor leading into the celestial room, I was walking several steps ahead of Grandpa when he stopped me, saying, 'Wait a moment, Allie. I want to tell you something. It was right here that the Lord Jesus Christ appeared to me at the time of the death of President Woodruff. He instructed me to go right ahead and reorganize the First Presidency of the Church at once and not wait as had been done after the death of the previous presidents, and that I was to succeed President Woodruff.'

"Then Grandpa came a step nearer and held out his left hand and said, 'He stood right here, about three feet above the floor. It looked as though he stood on a plate of solid gold.'

"Grandpa told me what a glorious personage the Savior is and described his hands, feet, countenance and beautiful white robes, all of which were of such glory of whiteness and brightness that he could hardly gaze upon him.

"Then Grandpa came another step nearer me and put his right hand on my head and said: 'Now, Granddaughter, I want you to remember that this is the testimony of your grandfather, that he told you with his own lips that he actually saw the Savior here in the temple and talked with him face to face.'

"Then we went on and Grandpa let me out of the main front door of the temple."

Deseret News, Church Section, April 2, 1938, pp. 3-8.

ADMITTED INTO HIS PRESENCE
Newel K. Knight

On the first day of June 1830, the first conference was held by the Church. Our number consisted of about thirty, besides many others who came to learn of our principles, or were already believers but had not been baptized. Having opened the meeting by singing and prayer, we partook of the emblems of the body and blood of our Lord Jesus Christ. A number were confirmed who had lately been baptized, and several were called and ordained to various offices in the priesthood. Much good instruction was given, and the Holy Ghost was poured out upon us in a marvelous manner. Many prophesied, while others had the heavens opened to their view. It was a scene long to be remembered. I felt my heart filled with love, with glory, and with pleasure unspeakable. I could discern all that was going on in the room and a vision of futurity also suddenly burst upon me, and I saw represented the great work which, through the instrumentality of Joseph Smith, was to be accomplished. I saw the heavens opened, I beheld the Lord Jesus Christ seated at the right hand of the Majesty on High, and it was made plain to my understanding that the time would come when I should be admitted into his presence, to enjoy his society for ever and ever.

Such scenes as these were calculated to inspire the hearts of the Saints with joy unspeakable, and fill us with awe and reverence for that Almighty Being by whose grace we had been called and made the happy partakers of such glorious blessings as were poured out upon us.

Newel Knight, "Newel Knight's Journal," *Scraps of Biography* (Fourth book of the Faith-Promoting Series, Salt Lake City: Juvenile Instructor Office, 1883), pp. 52-53.

DREAMS

The Lord does communicate some things of importance to the children of men by means of visions and dreams as well as by the records of divine truth. And what is it all for? It is to teach us a principle. We may never see anything take place exactly as we see it in a dream or a vision, yet it is intended to teach us a principle.

—Wilford Woodruff, *Journal of Discourses,* 22:333

THE LORD WORKS IN MYSTERIOUS WAYS
Edna Ogden

In 1949, my husband, Dale, and I were comfortably settled in Richfield, Utah, operating a large cattle and sheep ranch. Life was good—we had everything we needed to make us happy and content, except for a large family. I was unable to have any more children, which was a great disappointment to both of us. However, the longing and desire for another baby was still there. I found it impossible to pass by any baby without first stopping to admire a precious little soul that had just recently come from our Heavenly Father's presence.

I tried to be content as I spent my time caring for the three children we had and assisting Dale in his work as a stake missionary. There had been some discussion on dividing the stake mission and assigning half of the missionaries to work with the Navajo Indians who were beginning to come to Richfield to help with the harvesting of the sugar beets and other crops. The Korean War was on and it was extremely difficult to get farm laborers, so the farmers were delighted to have the Indians in the valley.

However, the changeover from their usual farm laborers to employing the Indians occurred so quickly that the farmers were unable to provide adequately for the Indians, so their situation was sad indeed. They were uneducated, ill-clothed for this type of weather, and their living conditions were deplorable. It was heart-rending to witness their pitiful plight.

As time went on, Dale and I became as concerned about the Indians' temporal well-being as we were over their spiritual salvation, and we began praying for inspiration and assistance in helping these Lamanite brothers and sisters with *all* of their needs.

Then, one night my Grandfather Rasmussen appeared to me in a dream. He was holding a baby in his arms and all I could see of the baby was a little head with a mop of thick black hair. He held the baby out towards me and said, "I have a baby for you."

"Oh, I'm so happy!" I exclaimed. "I hope it's a little girl!"

"Well, no," he said, "it's a boy."

"I don't want any more boys! I need a little girl," I replied.

He looked so very disappointed and then he said, "Well, all right, if that's the way you feel about it. I'll find someone else that will want this baby." He then turned and started to walk out the door.

"No! No! I didn't mean it!" I exclaimed. "I'll take the baby. I want the baby."

I was so distressed over his leaving with the baby that I awakened myself by calling out after him. The dream was over and Grandfather and the baby were gone, but their memory stayed very vividly with me for days. It was only a dream, but it seemed more like an experience. I felt as though I had actually visited with my grandfather.

Several days later I answered the phone and the voice at the other end said, "Hello. Is this the Dale Ogden residence?"

"Yes."

"Well, I'm calling from the hospital and we have a baby. . . ."

"I'll be right down!" I interrupted.

I knew instantly that this was the baby I saw in the dream. I had no doubt about it. I immediately went to the store and bought some diapers and baby clothes and then went to the hospital to take *my* baby home.

The nurse at the hospital, who was also serving as a stake missionary, said that the baby was a little Indian boy that had been brought to the hospital by his aunt. The Indians are very superstitious and do not believe in hospitals. When it appears that one of their own is about to die, they put them out of the home and let them die alone and with dignity. The baby had been very ill so the aunt, Flora Butler, who had been living with a family in Richfield and was more accustomed to our ways of treating the sick, had taken the baby and placed it in the hospital. The nurse further explained that the baby was now well enough to leave the hospital, but the parents could not be located. They had moved from the farm where they had been working and no one seemed to know at which farm they were staying. She had called my husband, since he was working with the Indians and could probably locate the parents.

I took the baby home and when my husband came home that night I rushed out to the truck to greet him. "Come into the house and see what we've got," I said.

He was astonished! He knew how badly I wanted another baby, so he didn't say much. He just quietly began trying to find the baby's parents.

In the meantime, I just enjoyed every minute of loving and caring for that precious baby. But in spite of my loving care, the baby became very ill and I had to take him back to the hospital. After examining the baby, the doctors told me that his canned milk formula wasn't agreeing with him and that he needed a new formula called Similac, if he was to live. We immediately called my husband's brother, Ross, who was a physician in Los Angeles, and he sent us a whole case of Similac.

The baby was able to tolerate the Similac, although he could take only very small amounts at a time and had to be fed about every hour, around the clock. He seemed to be gaining strength so we took him home and continued to care for him.

Dale located the parents and they came to the house to take their baby home. We explained the baby's health problems and informed them that he had to have a special formula and gave them what remained of the case of Similac. But they declined the Similac, saying, "If we take him, he will die. It would be better for him if you kept him."

So, we agreed to keep the baby. I was ecstatic! However, I didn't dare tell them that I knew all along the baby would someday be mine.

The baby still needed constant medical attention, so I took our little Bill to a friend of ours who was a doctor. "Don't keep this baby," he advised. "I know you have wanted more children and if you want a baby bad enough to adopt one, I'll find you another baby. This baby will never be healthy," he continued. "Look at him—his little legs and body are just like a raw piece of meat from the effects of the acid dysentery. If you think he looks bad on the outside, what do you think he looks like on the inside? His stomach doesn't have any lining and he'll never be able to eat anything but baby food. And, he'll probably never have any teeth and may have a total hearing loss because of the complications he's had from pneumonia! So," he said, "please don't keep *this* baby. If you want a baby, I'll get you one."

"But I *have* this one," I replied.

The doctor just shook his head. He didn't know what I knew —*this* was the baby the Lord wanted me to have.

I kept the baby. We put his name in the temple and invited the missionaries to join our family in fasting and prayer.

I continued giving the baby the Similac and before long he was retaining it well and started gaining weight. His skin healed in a matter of a week or two and I was able to put clothes on him. By the time he was ten months old he weighed a whopping twenty-five pounds. There wasn't anything he couldn't eat—he seemed to have a "cast-iron" stomach. He has a perfect set of beautiful white teeth, and has never had a filling. And his hearing is perfect, too.

He was the most adorable baby you ever saw. His "mother" loved him, but so did everyone else. Everywhere I took him, people would stop to comment on what an exceptionally beautiful baby he was.

When they organized the missionary program for the Lamanite people, Dale was set apart as the mission president and I was asked to serve on a stake mission. The Indians, however, were not receptive to discussing anything with the white man, including the gospel. They didn't trust any white man and preferred to have as little contact with us as possible. Thus, the missionaries were having a difficult time trying to find Lamanite families that would listen to their message of the restored gospel.

Every Sunday morning, Dale and I would take Bill and drive out to one of the farms where we knew some Indians would be camped. They were so startled to see us with an Indian baby that they would set aside their usual restraint and gather around us and ask questions. They found it hard to believe that we could care enough about the Indian people that we would actually take an Indian baby into our home to raise and to love. They were completely bewildered and confused, but pleased.

As soon as we could see that we had gained their confidence and respect, we would then invite them to Sunday school. We were delighted at the large numbers that were willing to come with us. Following the abbreviated Sunday School we would then present a cottage meeting, and before long many of them were receiving the discussions from the stake missionaries.

The work progressed beautifully—almost miraculously. One of the great joys of our life was to see many of these Lamanites join the Church. The Lord had truly answered our prayers and opened the way for us to help these deprived Indian people, spiritually at least.

We continued our missionary labors among the Lamanite people until the crops were harvested and they returned to their winter homes. However, our work with the Indians continued, but in a different manner. President Golden R. Buchanan arranged for several young Indian girls to spend the winter in Richfield so they could receive an education. The good people of Richfield opened their hearts and their homes to these young Indian girls, and along with five other families we gratefully accepted this opportunity. So, Frances Polacca, a delightful eleven-year-old Navajo from Crystal, New Mexico, joined our family. Thus, the Indian Student Placement Program began—a beautiful, inspired program of the Church to meet the temporal needs of our Lamanite brothers and sisters.[1]

It was a choice experience to have Frances in our home. She was truly an answer to our prayers in which we had asked for the opportunity to assist these Indian people both spiritually and temporally.

---

[1]See "Will the Saints Take Them into Their Homes?" p. 168.

During this time I was asked to have Frances and the other Indian girls participate in a sacrament meeting, so I gathered them into my home and we prepared a program. The following Sunday evening each one of the girls bore their simple but sincere testimonies. Following their talks, they sang, "We Thank Thee, O God, for a Prophet," as only the Indians can sing—from the depths of their souls. There wasn't a dry eye in the room. Everyone in the congregation was so touched and moved by this experience that they opened their hearts, and their homes, to the Lamanite people. We were flooded with requests for Indians to stay in LDS homes. We also received a great many requests for the girls to repeat their program in sacrament meetings in the stake and soon we were traveling to sacrament meetings in every part of the state. Each time the results were the same—the Saints would then welcome the Lamanite students into their homes. Within a very short time, hundreds of young Indian boys and girls were living in good LDS homes and receiving the education they needed so desperately.

We were thrilled at the way the Indian program was progressing and were enjoying every minute of our work with the Lamanite people. We had been blessed with everything we wanted—a large family, a thriving business, and an opportunity to really serve these suffering, deprived people. All in all, it was a very good life.

Then Ross asked us to come to Los Angeles and go into a business partnership with him and operate a carpet store. "No, thank you," we replied. "We're very happy with our life in Richfield. We've put our roots down here and we intend to stay."

The next time we went to Los Angeles for one of my periodical medical check-ups, Ross again broached the subject of our joining him in the carpet business. It just didn't seem to occur to him that we could possibly resist this marvelous opportunity, but we did. "Absolutely no!" we said. "We're not going to move!"

We returned to Richfield where, for some reason, we completely changed our attitude, and within two weeks we had moved into the Encino Ward in the San Fernando Valley. We were puzzled as to why the Lord would have us leave a good business of our own and go to another area where we couldn't continue our work with the Lamanites, whom we dearly loved. But, since we felt that it was what we should do, we settled into a different way of life in Southern California.

Frances had married and returned to the reservation to live, but we took Bill with us. Our Indian boy was quite a shock for some people, but he was so adorable that no one could resist him. Everyone in the ward and the stake adored him almost as much as we did. He continued to grow and develop into one of the finest young men any parent could hope for. He was truly a perfect representative and example for his people.

The Indian Student Placement Program continued to expand in Utah and soon several thousand young Indian boys and girls were participating in this wonderful program. Then word was received that the Placement Program would be extended into California and the stake selected to begin the program was Reseda Stake—the one Bill had grown up in. The saints in Reseda Stake responded warmly to this opportunity. How could they have done otherwise after having such a good experience with the only Lamanite most of them had ever known?

We knew then why we had to come to Southern California. We thought we had left our work with the Lamanite people behind, but the Lord again used us to fulfill his plans for his Lamanite sons and daughters.

I cannot bear to think of the many rich and choice blessings we would have missed had we not taken that Indian baby into our home. Little did I realize when my grandfather offered me that little baby boy the great joy that would come into our lives because of him and the great work that would then be done with the Lamanite people. The Lord does work in mysterious ways.

UNHARMED BY SERPENTS
President Wilford Woodruff

In the early days of the Church, it was a great treat to an elder in his travels through the country to find a Mormon; it was so with us. We were hardly in Arkansas when we heard of a family named Akeman. They were in Jackson County in the persecutions. Some of the sons had been tied up there and whipped on their bare backs with hickory switches by the mob. We heard of their living on Petit Jean River, in the Arkansas Territory, and we went a long way to visit them. . . . We arrived . . . within five miles of

Mr. Akeman's and were kindly entertained by a stranger. During the night I had the following dream:

I thought an angel came to us, and told us we were commanded of the Lord to follow a certain straight path, which was pointed out to us, let it lead us wherever it might. After we had walked in it awhile, we came to the door of a house, which was in the line of a high wall running north and south, so that we could not go around. I opened the door and saw the room was filled with large serpents, and I shuddered at the sight. My companion said he would not go into the room for fear of the serpents. I told him I should try to go through the room though they killed me, for the Lord had commanded it. As I stepped into the room, the serpents coiled themselves up, raised their heads some two feet from the floor, to spring at me. There was one much larger than the rest in the center of the room, which raised its head nearly as high as mine and made a spring at me. At that instant I felt as though nothing but the power of God could save me, and I stood still. Just before the serpent reached me, he dropped dead at my feet; all the rest dropped dead, swelled up, turned black, burst open, took fire and were consumed before my eyes, and we went through the room unharmed, and thanked God for our deliverance.

I awoke in the morning and pondered upon the dream. We took breakfast and started on our journey on Sunday morning, to visit Mr. Akeman. I related to my companion my dream, and told him we should see something strange. We had great anticipations of meeting Mr. Akeman, supposing him to be a member of the Church. When we arrived at his house, he received us very coldly, and we soon found that he had apostatized. He brought railing accusations against the Book of Mormon and the Authorities of the Church.

Word was sent through all the settlements on the river for twenty miles that two Mormon preachers were in the place. A mob was soon raised, and warning sent to us to leave immediately or we would be tarred and feathered, ridden on a rail and hanged. I soon saw where the serpents were. My companion wanted to leave; I told him no, I would stay and see my dream fulfilled.

There was an old gentleman and lady named Hubbel, who had read the Book of Mormon and believed. Father Hubbel came to see us, and invited us to make our home with him while we stayed in the place. We did so, and labored for him some three weeks with our axes, clearing land, while we were waiting to see the salvation of God.

I was commanded of the Lord by the Holy Ghost to go and warn Mr. Akeman to repent of his wickedness. I did so, and each time he railed against me, and the last time he ordered me out of his house. When I went out he followed me, and was very angry. When he came up to me, about eight rods from the house, he fell dead at my feet, turned black and swelled up, as I saw the serpents do in my dream.

His family, as well as ourselves, felt it was the judgment of God upon him. I preached his funeral sermon. Many of the mob died suddenly. We stayed about two weeks after Akeman's death and preached, baptized Mr. Hubbel and his wife, and then continued on our journey.

Wilford Woodruff, *Leaves from My Journal* (Third book of the Faith-Promoting Series, Salt Lake City: Juvenile Instructor Office, 1882), pp. 13-15.

THE LORD FULFILLS MY FONDEST DREAMS

Dr. Sami Hanna

When I left my native land of Egypt in 1955 to come to this country as a Fulbright Scholar, I had never heard of the LDS Church. I was somewhat acquainted with many of the denominations of this country, but I had never heard of the Mormons.

My first contact with the Church came just a few days after my arrival in New York. I was alone in my hotel room on Sunday morning, so I turned the radio on for company. I had tuned in just in time to hear Richard L. Evans introduce the program by saying that the music would be presented by "the Tabernacle Choir from the Crossroads of the West." The choir was obviously carefully trained and the music was beautiful and quite comforting for lonely Sundays in New York, so I made a mental note of where the station was and the time of the broadcast. For the next three years, the Tabernacle Choir from Salt Lake City became my unfailing companion on Sunday mornings.

In 1958 I was offered a fellowship at the University of Illinois, so I moved to Urbana where I continued my activities for two years. After I had been there a year, I received a letter from Dr. Assiz Atiya, a former professor of mine during my college days in Egypt. He was now affiliated with the University of Utah in Salt Lake City and wrote urging me to join him on the faculty to help build up the Arabic program at the University of Utah.

I showed the letter to my department chairman and asked him what he thought about it, and he said, "No! No! I wouldn't go to Salt Lake or *anywhere* in Utah."

"Why?" I asked.

"Because," he mumbled, "it's not that the University is all that bad and dreadful, it's just that the Mormons live there."

"Oh! What are the Mormons?" I asked. "Are they people like us, or just what are they?"

"Well," he answered, "they're one of *those* sects, and it just happens that my wife is a Mormon so I know all about them and I wouldn't advise you to go back there."

And so I wrote back to Professor Atiya and told him that my chairman was really not in favor of my coming so I would prefer to remain in Urbana. Then he wrote back again, and thinking that I could be enticed by a more attractive offer, offered to raise my salary.

Again I went to the chairman to ask what he thought about my accepting this generous offer. He responded by offering to match any salary offered by the University of Utah. I was enjoying my work at Urbana, and with this last turn of events I could see no compelling reason to leave Urbana and go to Salt Lake City, so I again declined the position.

Professor Atiya continued to write to me for the following year, urging me to come to the University of Utah. Finally, convinced that I was really needed to help bolster the Arabic Studies program at the University of Utah, I agreed to come to Salt Lake City for one year if Professor Atiya would take the responsibility of obtaining my chairman's approval and release from my studies at Urbana. Consequently, my chairman received a letter requesting my services for only a one-year period, to which he no longer objected.

Thus, in September of 1960, I packed my bags and came to the "Crossroads of the West," Salt Lake City, to see what the West and those curious Mormons were like. I was rather startled to find the landscape and scenery so totally unlike that of my homeland of Egypt, which is very flat and very arid. The mountains and canyons were exceptionally beautiful and magnificent and the people of Salt Lake were as impressive as their surroundings. Their warmth was just overwhelming, and I soon found that all of my Mormon colleagues were really not as dreadful as I had been led to believe, but were in reality living examples of a Christianity that teaches brotherly love. Because of the great friendship shown me, I began to make my associations more with the Mormons than any other group and soon became fast friends with Dr. Faust, the brother of Elder James E. Faust, Assistant to the Twelve. My work at the University was challenging and rewarding and my association with my Mormon colleagues was so comfortable that the one-year period that I was on loan from the University of Illinois came and went and I was still in Salt Lake City. Another year came and went and I found myself quite contented to remain among the Mormon people and to imitate their way of life.

Time went by, and my admiration for the Mormon people and their church continued to grow. I was so very impressed by the dedication and service of all Church members, of *all* stations. I was rather amazed to find that members of the Church who were financially well established, and even members of the "hierarchy" of the Church, would give of their precious time free of charge to work on farms picking vegetables, canning food and other menial chores. I was so impressed by this love and dedication to the Church and concern for the well-being of their fellowmen that I too wanted to join in and assist in these programs, even though I was not a member. I was told to be patient, that the time would come when I would be called upon to participate in the Welfare Program.

Still wanting to do something for the Church, one day I asked Dr. Streadbeck, the Foreign Advisor at the University, if the Church had as yet published any materials in Arabic for the missionaries. He replied that he didn't know and would check with the Church officials. He called Elder Gordon B. Hinckley and was told that the Church had just started sending missionaries into Arabic-speaking countries. Elder Hinckley stated that the missionaries would, of course, be far more effective if they could be supplied with Church literature in Arabic and expressed his appreciation for the opportunity to have this accomplished.

Delighted with the possibility of serving the Church, I told Dr. Streadbeck that I would take the first tract, *The Joseph Smith Story,* and translate it into Arabic. After many enjoyable hours at my Arabic typewriter, I had the translation completed and excitedly made an appointment with Elder Hinckley to present my work to the Church. Dr. Streadbeck had also made arrangements to accompany me to Elder Hinckley's office. Shortly before our scheduled appointment, he said to me, "Sami, before we go into Elder Hinckley's office and give this pamphlet to him, why don't you join the Church?"

I had greatly admired the Mormon people and their church for some time, but the possibility of actually *joining* the Church had never been a part of my thinking. I was totally unprepared for this question and didn't really know what to say, so I put him off with a comment that I had wondered about many things concerning the Church, but I just wasn't ready for it. I reminded him that I had completed the translation of the Joseph Smith tract *only* because I loved the Church and desired to be of service to those about me, and not because I was trying to "earn" membership in the Church.

However, the suggestion that I join the Church began to ferment in my mind and I began to study the Church with a seriousness and earnest desire to know if the Church was really true. I felt that if I was going to learn more about the Church, I should at least be attending the Church services, so I asked Dr. Streadbeck if I could attend with him. He seemed pleased with my request and replied that I could indeed attend his ward. So, every Sunday for over a year, I attended his ward, which was several miles from my home, and I sat in on Dr. Streadbeck's class, which I found very stimulating and informative.

About this time, the Church Authorities approached me with a request to translate the Book of Mormon into Arabic. I hesitated to undertake the project until I knew something more about the Book of Mormon, for I had reservations about rendering simply a literal translation. I wanted to be able to convey the spirit of the book and that I couldn't do until I had studied the Book of Mormon in depth. I inquired around and was told that the LDS Institute offered a course of the Book of Mormon. I was given the name of the instructor, and subsequently asked him if I could sit in on his class since I was going to be doing a translation of it for the Church and wanted to know more about the book first. He graciously consented. On my first day in class the instructor introduced me, informing the class of my reason for attending, and then added the footnote that I was not a Church member.

Then circumstances started working towards that end. I began to feel that I was living in a vacuum. I had experienced some success in the academic community and had published extensively, but I began to ask myself, "Am I here on earth only to publish and to teach?" I wanted to do something for humanity, to belong to something that would fill this huge gap in my life. With this on my mind, I began to talk to Dean Tyler about Church membership —would it give more meaning to life and help fill this void of service to humanity that I felt so desperately? He replied that the Mormon Church is a very difficult church, very demanding. I told him that was what I loved about the Church. He continued to encourage me, and yet I felt a reluctance to make that final commitment.

This period of indecision continued until one night in May of 1973 when I had a very strange dream. I dreamed that I was in the foyer of a chapel which was identical in architecture and beauty to the Yale Ward building that was across the street from the duplex in which I lived. A large number of people that I had never met were leaving the chapel, apparently at the conclusion of a service. I found that a man had taken my right hand and a lady was holding me by my left hand. They assisted me down the stairs and then the lady left and I found myself alone with the gentleman. He took me out of the chapel and I followed him into the parking lot area. But I didn't see the parking lot; in my dream I saw just a small running river. The man with me said nothing; he only pointed to the water and as he did so, the words, "There it is!" were impressed upon my mind.

I immediately awoke, quite bewildered and confused by the experience, for this was not an ordinary dream, but a very strange experience I didn't understand. I've had dreams before, but none were like this one—so vivid that the memory of it seemed to be burned upon all my senses. This was a special dream—one that had to have a special meaning or purpose, but what was it? I was so emotionally charged that I felt that I had to have the answer immediately, so I phoned Dr. Faust and asked if he had a few minutes to talk about the Church. He replied, "Sure! Come on over."

I greeted him with, "Do you believe in dreams?"

"Of course we do," he replied. "What was your dream about?"

"Well, it was the strangest dream I've ever had in my whole life," I explained. "I've been here in Salt Lake for thirteen years and I've never had such a dream."

"Well, tell me about it," he encouraged.

I then related the dream to him and concluded by asking him, "Do you think this is an invitation from the Lord to join this Church?"

"I would say yes, and I would take it very seriously," he said.

I did take it seriously, and began to think positively about joining the Church. I had loved the Church for years and had suppressed my desires for Church membership as there were special problems involved. But after the dream I could no longer comfortably ignore or suppress these hopes that had been so stirred up. A few days later I met with the bishop, the late Bishop Joseph Smith, Jr., to discuss my desires for joining the Church. The bishop responded that he would be glad to have me as I would be an asset to the Church, and quoted scriptures to support his position that I would be welcome.

I no longer hesitated and a date was hurriedly set for my baptism into the Church, as I was due to leave for Tunisia in a few days. I regretfully went alone to my baptism, for none of the other members of my family had a desire to join the Church. I had expected it to be a joyous but lonely experience, but, much to my surprise, I found all of my colleagues there, as well as all of my neighbors. To add to my joy, I suddenly realized that the chapel I was in, which I had never been in before, was identical to the one I had seen in my dream! I no longer had any doubts or reservations that the Lord had desired my baptism and that I was doing the right thing in joining the Mormon Church.

Many new horizons and opportunities to serve my fellowmen have opened to me since my baptism. Besides having the choice experience of translating the Book of Mormon into Arabic, I see that more of the Church literature should be translated into Arabic, a task which I feel so privileged to undertake.

The Lord knew that I needed to be baptized to bring about the fulfillment of my fondest dreams, but he also knew that if I were to accomplish this, I needed the prodding and assurance that he provided in his special dream to me, for which I shall be eternally grateful.

HE WANTS US

Lorenzo Dow Young

In the autumn of 1816, when about nine years old, I had a peculiar dream. I thought I stood in an open, clear space of ground, and saw a plain, fine road, leading at an angle of forty-five degrees into the air, as far as I could see. I heard a noise like a carriage in rapid motion, at what seemed the upper end of the road. In a moment it came in sight. It was drawn by a pair of beautiful white horses. The carriage and harness appeared brilliant with gold. The horses traveled with the speed of the wind. It was made manifest to me that the Savior was in the carriage, and that it was driven by his servant. The carriage stopped near me, and the Savior inquired where my brother Brigham was. After informing him, he further inquired about my other brothers, and our father. After I had answered his inquiries, he stated that he wanted us all, but he especially wanted my brother Brigham. The team then turned right about and returned on the road it had come.

I awoke at once, and slept no more that night. I felt frightened, and supposed we were all going to die. I saw no other solution to the dream. It was a shadowing of our future which I was then in no condition to discern.

In the morning I told my father the dream, and my fears that we were going to die. He comforted me with the assurance that he did not think my interpretation was correct.

Lorenzo Dow Young, "Lorenzo Dow Young's Narrative," *Fragments of Experience* (Sixth book of the Faith-Promoting Series, Salt Lake City: Juvenile Instructor Office, 1882), pp. 23-24.

THE APPEARANCE OF PLENTY

Elder Heber C. Kimball

One night (about 1838), while at the village of Rochester (England), I dreamed that I, in company with another person, was walking out, and saw a very extensive field of wheat, more so than the eye could reach. Such a sight I never before witnessed. The wheat appeared to be perfectly ripe, and ready for harvest. I was very much rejoiced at the glorious sight which presented itself, but judge of my surprise when, on taking some of the ears and rubbing them in my hands, I found nothing but smut. I marveled exceedingly, and felt very sorrowful, and exclaimed, "What will the people do for grain; here is a great appearance of plenty, but there is no sound wheat!"

While contemplating the subject, I looked in another direction, and saw a small field in the form of the letter L, which had the appearance of something growing in it. I immediately directed my steps to it, and found that it had been sown with wheat, some of which had grown about six inches high, other parts of the field not quite so high, and some had only just sprouted. This gave me great encouragement to expect that at the harvest there would be some good grain. While thus engaged, a large bull, very fierce and angry, leaped over the fence, ran through the field, and stamped down a large quantity of that which had just sprouted, and after doing considerable injury he leaped over the fence and ran away.

I felt very much grieved that so much wheat should be destroyed, when there was such a prospect of scarcity. When I awoke next morning, the interpretation was given me. The large field with the great appearance of grain, so beautiful to look upon, represented the nation in which I then resided, which had a very pleasing appearance and a great show of religion, and made great pretensions to piety and godliness, but denied the power thereof. It was destitute of the principles of truth, and consequently of the gifts of the spirit.

The small field I saw clearly represented the region of country where I was laboring, and where the word of truth had taken root and was growing in the hearts of those who had the gospel, some places having grown a little more than others. The village I was in was that part of the field where the bull did so much injury, for during my short visit there most of the inhabitants were believing, but as soon as I departed, a clergyman belonging to the Church of England came out and violently attacked the truth, and made considerable noise, crying, "False prophet! delusion!" and after trampling on truth and doing all the mischief he could before I returned, he took shelter in his pulpit. However, he did not destroy all the seed, for after my return I was instrumental in building up a church in that place.

Heber C. Kimball, *Heber C. Kimball's Journal* (Seventh book of the Faith-Promoting Series, Salt Lake City: Juvenile Instructor Office, 1882), pp. 41-43.

FAITH

What the world needs today more than anything else is an implicit faith in God, our Father, and in Jesus Christ, his Son, as the Redeemer of the world.

—Heber J. Grant, *CR,* April 1935, p. 9

THE REWARDS OF FAITH
Robert L. Richards

The big event for all collegiate track team members is the National Collegiate Athletic Association championship races, which in 1966 were held in Bloomington, Indiana. BYU's coach, Clarence Robison, felt that it was important for the team to be thoroughly adjusted to the differences in altitude and climate, so we arrived in Terre Haute one week earlier to compete in the United States Track and Field Federation championships.

This was only my third time to compete in the steeplechase. At this time I couldn't judge distance or keep my pace over the hurdles, so I had to chop my steps, lose momentum, then jump straight up and down over them. To overcome this handicap I ran my heart out between hurdles. Then, with a lap and a half to go, I struck my right knee on a hurdle. It was extremely painful and I wanted to stop, but I just couldn't that close to the end of the race. The knee began swelling almost immediately and was beginning to lock up by the time the finish line was in sight. But, in spite of that knee, I kept on running, and won!

My knee was examined at the University's clinic where it was determined that no bones were broken, but there was some internal bleeding and damage. "It will be at least a month before you can run again," the doctor said.

That hit me so hard I couldn't believe it! Receiving the championship crown in the Federation race wasn't worth it. The most important meet was the NCAA—that was what it was all about. The dreams and years of training for this one event were dashed and shattered! I was heartsick! And so was the coach. I can still remember the look of disappointment on Coach Robison's face when the doctor told him I wouldn't be running in the NCAA race. He couldn't easily replace me with another athlete from the squad. We were too far from home and no one else with the team had qualified for the NCAA.

The next day was Sunday, and since there was no Latter-day Saint Church in the area, we spent a quiet and personal day. I spent the day out of doors in communion with my Heavenly Father and it was one of the most spiritual days of my life. As I walked along the banks of the Wabash River thinking about my life, the Church and the principles that I had been taught in Primary and Sunday School, it came to me quite strongly that I needed a blessing from the priesthood. But for some reason it was difficult to ask for a blessing. Perhaps it was because I was beginning to question everything, instead of accepting things on faith as I had done as a child. I knew that I couldn't be a hypocrite and ask for a blessing just because it was the thing to do to keep my image as a good Mormon. I had to believe in it and *know* that my Heavenly Father would bless me. This was a real testing period for me as I spent that morning meditating and praying to my Father in heaven. I grew in belief and understanding as I received my answer. I knew that what I needed most, and wanted and *believed* in, was a blessing.

I returned to the motel and asked Coach Robison if he would give me a blessing, and of course he answered yes. What a fantastic opportunity this was to be on a university team and be able to turn to my coach, a man that has the power and the priesthood of our Father in heaven, and ask him for a blessing.

I asked two other team members to assist him and I was given a blessing, and a challenge. Coach Robison simply asked our Father in heaven to bless me and give me the strength to do his will. He didn't say that I would be healed or have the strength to run and win the race, or any of the things I wanted to hear. He just said, "Heavenly Father, bless Bob that he will be a fine representative of the Church, the University, his family and himself. And, if it be thy will, we pray that he will be returned to full health and strength and be able to compete."

The responsibility was back on my shoulders. I realize now that that was the way it should be. It would have been thrilling to have had Coach Robison say, "You will be healed instantly and returned to full health and strength. You have exercised sufficient faith, and for this you will be blessed." But that was not the way my Heavenly Father sought to help me to grow in faith and understanding. I had to find out my Heavenly Father's will and act accordingly, I spent the rest of that Sunday in prayer and meditation, and growing spiritually.

Monday we traveled to Bloomington, Indiana, for the NCAA. The meet was scheduled for Thursday, Friday, and Saturday, with the steeplechase race on Friday. My knee continued to be painful, so I followed the doctor's orders and didn't run and train with the rest of the team. Instead, I spent the next two days just walking in the wooded countryside, pouring out my heart to my Heavenly Father.

Thursday morning I went for another walk, but this time there was very little pain. I couldn't resist the urge so I tried jogging a little. Although it hurt, I could do it and maintain control. I went into a full run. Oh, it felt great to move that fast again! I didn't want to stop—I wanted to continue running and train all day, but I had to conserve my strength. I knew that I was ready to compete, and would actually be running in that race tomorrow.

I will never forget that night. I ran the steeplechase so many times in my mind I couldn't count them. They were for real, too, as I would be covered with sweat when I awakened—and I won them all! It was a relief when morning came.

I had another treatment on my knee just before going to the stadium Friday morning and a rub-down just before the race was to begin. I had victory on my mind, but in my heart I knew that I should be grateful to just be running. I offered a prayer that I might do my best as I walked slowly to that fateful starting line.

I planned to run the whole race fast and not to leave it to a final sprint, so I asked the coach to yell when he saw me falter or when my competitors started gaining on me. I wasn't going to look behind me, no matter what.

". . . Bill Norris, Boston College; Bob Price, California; Ken Moore, Oregon; William Reilly, Penn State; Jack Bacheler, Miami; Bob Richards, Brigham Young; . . ." came the announcement over the public address system. The gun fired. It was the greatest moment of my life.

I started a little fast, then settled into a stride as I took the lead. My first hurdle. Could I do it? Yes, it felt good! I had form and could follow through. I kept myself alert, thinking every moment. With just less than a mile to go, I called out to Coach Robison, "Are they gaining on me?"

"No," he answered, "you look fine."

The next lap, the same reply. I couldn't believe it! The other runners had to be making their move by now. Then I thought, if I were the coach I would also tell a runner that, even if it wasn't true, just to keep him psyched up. Since the track was rubberized, I couldn't hear or feel how close the others might be. So on the next lap I yelled, "Tell me the truth!" The reply was the same.

The final stretch. I picked up stride a little. The home stretch, the finish line—I was national collegiate champion! All-American! The thrill was even greater when I looked back to see my nearest competitor coming off the final turn some eighty yards behind me.

Stardom with all its glory unfolded. Newspaper reporters, picture taking, and offers of free track shoes from various companies became new and everyday experiences. It was all very exciting, but my thoughts were filled with gratitude to my Heavenly Father for his choice blessings. I trained for years to win that race, but in the end I had to give all the credit to my Heavenly Father. He was there when I needed him, and always will be if I just have faith in him.

The rewards of faith are rich. No greater blessing can a man possess than the great gift of faith.

FAITH IN THE TONGAN ISLANDS

Eric Shumway

On Wednesday evening, March 15, 1961, we were gathered at the mission house in Neiafu with some of the Tongan missionaries of the Vava'u District. It was a kind of farewell get together and sleep-in since I was being transferred to Tongatapu the following day.

As we were talking, we heard a "caller" making his way through the village. In a loud voice he was warning the people that a hurricane would hit Vava'u at about five o'clock the following morning. The missionaries, most of whom were married and had small children, did not seem too concerned about it because the warnings of hurricanes came in March every year.

But at two o'clock the next morning the wind began to blow. By five it was very strong. Two missionaries came into the house from where they were sleeping and asked me to take them back to their villages in the mission car. I agreed, but when I opened the door to look out I saw the trees already coming down. The road was completely blocked and nothing could get through. I told the missionaries it might be safer if they would walk.

Before they got out of sight, the wind became really violent. This is when I realized we were in for a great hurricane, not just one that they have every year, but one which would make history.

We called all the people who lived nearby and invited them to go into the chapel. We didn't want anyone to stay in the older buildings, since they might collapse at any moment. I figured that two of the houses on the lot would probably be taken in the wind.

About nine o'clock, everything in the town began going up. My Tongan companion and I stood out on the west side of the chapel (the wind was coming from the east) so we could see everything that went on in town. From where we stood, we could see houses being blown over and big trees torn up by their roots and thrown into the air. We could see the Wesleyan tabernacle, which is about a block from our chapel, being dismantled by invisible hands. We learned later that a man was crushed to death when the building collapsed. The Tongan Free Church tabernacle was also demolished.

At ten o'clock we estimated the wind to be about 150 miles an hour, an estimation that was later confirmed by the Tongan government.

Most of the houses which stood near our chapel were destroyed. The huge mango tree (a mango tree is comparable to the oak tree in America for strength) that stood across the street from our chapel was in ribbons. Large limbs, a foot in diameter, were torn off like match sticks and taken to the sea or dropped out in the road.

When the wind hit, we all noticed that Tonga Malohifo'ou was not at the chapel. Most of the Saints in the village and many nonmembers had come to our chapel for safety. As branch president, Brother Malohifo'ou should have been the first one there to help organize the "confusion." He didn't show up that morning or noon.

In America, President Malohifo'ou's little house would be called a wooden shack. Badly in need of repair, it was a fragile single frame structure built on four posts. It was far enough away from the chapel to make it very dangerous to go there in such wind.

That night he didn't show up at the chapel, and Friday morning he still wasn't there. About ten o'clock, the wind was still over a hundred miles an hour, but I couldn't restrain myself from trying to find him to see how his family was, for I loved them greatly. I asked Vili Pele to go with me and we ran to find President Malohifo'ou. When we reached his *api,* we were greatly surprised to see his house still standing, without any apparent damage, amid tons of debris. The Tongan Free Church tabernacle across the road had been razed. The large house that stood on the corner, very close to President Malohifo'ou's, had disappeared. The house on the other side of his *api* was completely demolished. The four vavae trees on his lot had fallen. But his little frame house still stood, and everything else on the lot was intact.

When we reached the house, I called to him to open the door. President Malohifo'ou had to brace himself against the door to let us in as the wind was still strong enough to take the door right off!

When we entered the house I thoroughly expected to see dead people. But his wife cheerfully called my name and invited us to sit down and eat some of the cold yam that they had eaten that morning. Again it surprised us that they had been able to build a fire and cook some food, for most of the people in Vava'u had been without food from Thursday through Friday morning.

The first thing I asked President Malohifo'ou was why he disregarded his position and did not go to the chapel with his wife. He didn't say anything, but just pointed to the little children on the floor. He told us he didn't dare go outside the house as one of them might have been killed. I told him I thought it would have been much better to try to go to the chapel than to stay there and be crushed to death in the house. He just smiled and said nothing.

When we persisted in asking him why he didn't make a break for the chapel, President Malohifo'ou began to weep and said, "Elder Shumway, I want you and Vili to come in here to this other room, and I'll tell you why I didn't go."

We went into the room and he said, "I've already told you why I didn't go. I was afraid to go outside. The wind hadn't really reached its peak, but I could hear the roof and feel the house shaking, as if it were ready to fall. I knew that if I stayed in the house I would die with my family, and if I went outside I'd die. At that time, I climbed up on this chair and I placed my hand right on the part of the roof I thought would go off first. I said, 'By the power of the priesthood which I hold, and in the name of Jesus Christ, I command you to stand solidly and completely throughout this storm.' I stopped the storm from this house, from this lot, and from these houses which stand on the lot."

President Malohifo'ou told us that after he had said these words, the house quit shaking, the roof quit rattling, the wind *seemed* to die down outside. But it hadn't. The wind *was* stopped from that little house, because he commanded it in the name of Jesus Christ and by the power of the priesthood!

For about five minutes Vili and I couldn't speak—couldn't say anything. Lumps were in my throat, and my heart was burning. We knew that the power of the Lord had been manifested.

Adapted from a compilation of interviews by Elder Vernon Tyler (copy on file in Brigham Young University Library, Provo, Utah), pp. 13-17; 22-26.

TAKE THE LORD AT HIS WORD
Gregory G. Vernon

During a particularly difficult period of my mission in Vancouver, British Columbia, I was engaged in a development conference with Bishop Albert Heath. I had a tremendous respect for Bishop Heath. He was a man of some means, the president of a large firm in British Columbia, and the bishop of his ward. He was also an erudite and accomplished speaker and delivered his message with great power and firm conviction when he spoke. His command of the English language was remarkable, as was his enthusiasm and dedication to the Church. Bishop Heath was an exceptional man—highly successful and affluent and yet a humble servant of the Lord whose exemplary life was worthy of serving as a model to each missionary for patterning his own life.

During this conference, the purpose of which was to obtain new referrals for the missionary program, Bishop Heath suddenly changed the subject matter of his discussion with us and referred to a section of the Doctrine and Covenants that contained one of the Lord's admonitions to missionaries of the early Church. The admonition was: "Take ye no thought for the morrow, for what ye shall eat, or what ye shall drink, . . . For your Father, who is in heaven, knoweth that you have need of all these things." (D&C 84:80, 83.)

After reading that section, he turned to us and asked if we believed what he had just read. Of course, we answered in the affirmative. And then he queried us as to whether we had put such a thing into practice. I responded by indicating to him that I did not know exactly what he meant.

Bishop Heath then challenged us to test the Lord and take him at his word and see whether or not he would fulfill the promises contained in the scriptures.

I was immediately and profoundly impressed by his statements and by the direction which he seemed to be imparting to me personally. I therefore firmly resolved to do my best to place my immediate earthly needs in the hands of the Lord. Of course, it was with some hesitancy that I did this, and I must admit that my faith did waver; however, I was firmly resolved to place the care and custody of my physical needs in the hands of him for whom I was employed.

A remarkable thing happened, and it happened almost immediately. My needs for bodily sustenance were met from outside quarters from that day on. The companion with whom I was laboring had been a party to our conversation with Bishop Heath and had also silently determined to put his faith in that scripture to the test. We did not spend so much as a dime on food or drink for the duration of our companionship from that point onward.

When we were transferred, my new companion, who had just entered the mission field, inquired of me as to what my monthly food budget was. Even though I made several excuses for not answering him, his interrogatories to me persisted, and I finally told him in all candor that I spent no money whatsoever on food, nor had I incurred any expenditures for bodily sustenance and physical needs for a period that was then several months in duration. Looking back on this experience, I am not sure that he believed me, but as the weeks and months passed and we had still not found it necessary to purchase any food, drink, clothing or other bodily needs, his faith became as clear and unwavering as mine.

Shortly thereafter, I was transferred several thousand miles north to the cold reaches of Alaska and there became companion to another elder who had been in the area for several weeks preceding my arrival. Again, one of his immediate concerns was for money for our food budget. And again, my responses to his inquiries were at first vague and noncommital.

Finally, after several days, I related to him my experience with Bishop Heath and told him that I believed that we would be provided for. I feel that my discussion with him affected him profoundly, and it seemed to me that his very countenance had been transformed. He, too, had been deeply touched by the Spirit and the admonition of the Lord to rely upon him for our daily needs and determined that he also would live as directed by the scriptures.

We then commenced our missionary activities with as much diligence as we could muster and were met with great and continuing success. In times past, prior to my sojourn to Alaska, I had been provided with food and clothing, as well as some other bodily needs, from sources which I considered to be divinely influenced. However, I must candidly admit that my efforts toward the missionary work were not 100 percent commitment-type efforts and that I was somewhat negligent in my duties and had not fulfilled my obligations to the best of my abilities. I had done nothing sinful or grievous in nature, but merely had not expended my best efforts on behalf of the Lord's work. However, that changed in Alaska, and we both put forth renewed and redoubled efforts to bring about success in our endeavors.

Not only were our efforts rewarded with numerous convert baptisms, but occurrences of unusual magnitude began to take place regularly. As we were tracting late one afternoon, we knocked on the door of a young man and his wife. They immediately invited us in, as many others had done, and after we had introduced ourselves, they stated that they were not particularly interested in hearing our message, but would very much like to have us stay and partake of a meal with them. It turned out that the gentleman was a roughneck who was employed on the offshore oil rigs in Alaska. He was a diver and during one of his trips to the ocean floor had caught a huge Alaska king crab, which subsequently turned out to be our dinner that evening. It was one of the most remarkable meals that I have ever enjoyed, before or since.

They invited us back the next night for another meal and as we were preparing to leave they informed us that they were going to California for the remainder of the winter. They stated that they had paid six months' rent in advance, and had stocked the pantry with a generous supply of food. They then proceeded to hand us the keys to the house and insisted that we stay in their home, at no expense, while they were gone. We were flattered, pleased, and humbled at their offer and accepted it with much thankfulness.

During the rest of our stay in the north country, every one of our earthly needs was met. Our food was supplied, both by the generous people I have just spoken of and by other people that we would meet, *without* making any solicitation. We deliberately and consciously made an effort not to solicit food, meals, or anything else. Nevertheless, each and every day, as we went about our duties and pursued the work of the Lord in that area, we would regularly be fed by those people we contacted, most of whom were strangers and merely responded to our knock at their door. An unusual number of them were interested in our message and we found that there were many days when our tracting inquiries were favorably received by each and every person whom we contacted. Our needs for clothing were met from unexpected sources and our housing was taken care of by persons who were not even members of the Church, and, to the best of my knowledge, never became members of the Church.

It was of profound and lasting inspiration to me that a period in excess of eighteen months elapsed during which neither myself nor my companions expended so much as a dime for food or clothing, and, for the last several months of that time, made no expenditure for housing or shelter. Our faith was constantly and continually rewarded. We had proven the Lord and came to receive the benefits of the promises given in the scriptures.

I TRUSTED IN GOD
Philo Dibble

When Joseph Smith first came to Nauvoo, then called Commerce, a Mr. White, living there, proffered to sell him his farm for twenty-five hundred dollars, five hundred dollars of the amount to be paid down, and the balance one year from that time. Joseph and the brethren were talking about this offer when some of them said, "We can't buy it, for we lack the money." Joseph took out his purse, and emptying out its contents, offered a half dollar to one of the brethren, which he declined accepting, but Joseph urged him to take it, and then gave each of the other brethren a similar amount, which left him without any. Addressing the brethren, he then said, "Now you all have money and I have none; but the time will come when I will have money and you will have none!" He then said to Bishop Knight, "You go back and buy that farm!"

Brother Knight went to White, but learned from him that he had raised the price one hundred dollars, and returned to Joseph without closing the bargain. Joseph again sent him with positive orders to purchase, but Brother Knight, finding that White had raised the price still another hundred dollars, again returned without purchasing. For the third time then, Joseph commanded him to go and buy the farm, and charged him not to come back till he had done so.

When Bishop Knight got back to White, he had raised another hundred on the place, making the whole amount twenty-eight hundred dollars. However, the bargain was closed and the obligations drawn up, but how the money was going to be raised neither Brother Knight nor the other brethren could see. The next morning Joseph and several of the brethren went down to Mr. White's to sign the agreement and make the first payment on the land. A table was brought out with the papers upon it, and Joseph signed them, moved back from the table and sat with his head down as if in thought for a moment. Just then a man drove up in a carriage and asked if Mr. Smith was there. Joseph, hearing it, got up and went to the door. The man said, "Good morning, Mr. Smith; I am on a speculation today. I want to buy some land, and thought I could come and see you." Joseph then pointed around where his land lay, but the man said, "I can't go with you today to see the land. Do you want any money this morning?"

Joseph replied that he would like some, and when the stranger asked, "How much?" he told him, "Five hundred dollars."

The man walked into the house with Joseph, emptied a small sack of gold on the table, and counted out that amount. He then handed to Joseph another hundred dollars, saying, "Mr. Smith, I make you a present of this."

After this transpired, Joseph laughed at the brethren and said, "You trusted in money; but I trusted in God. Now I have money, and you have none."

Early Scenes in Church History (Eighth book of the Faith-Promoting Series, Salt Lake City: Juvenile Instructor Office, 1882), pp. 95-96.

DON'T TRY TO KILL THAT MAN

Day after day Benjamin Franklin Johnson's life was threatened by the Missouri mobsters. His captors would frequently warn him, "We'll kill you tomorrow sure, and in a way to make you yell right smart." The following, which he related many years later, tells of one attempt a guard made to carry out his threats:

While sitting upon a log one day, a brute came to him with a rifle in hand, saying, "You give up Mormonism right now, or I'll shoot you."

Receiving a decisive refusal, he took deliberate aim not ten feet distant and pulled the trigger. No explosion occurred, and he cursed fearfully, saying he had used the gun twenty years and it had never before missed fire.

He examined the lock, put in fresh priming and again essayed to shoot Johnson, but without effect, and a third time with the same result.

A bystander told him to fix up his gun a little, and then, said he, "You can kill the cuss all right."

"Yes," said the would-be murderer, "I'll put in a fresh load."

He did so, and again essayed to kill Johnson. This time the gun burst and killed the wretch upon the spot, and a bystander was heard to say, "You'd better not try to kill that man."

Deseret Evening News, December 19, 1905, p. 4.

FASTING

Miracles are brought about through fasting and sincere prayer.

—Elder Henry D. Taylor, from an address delivered at the 144th Semiannual General Conference, October 1974

MOTHERLY FEELINGS
Elder "W"

Our mission president encouraged the missionaries to live in the homes of nonmember families rather than renting an apartment. The reason for this was to provide a home atmosphere where the elders could have good nourishing meals prepared for them by the lady of the household, and, more importantly, it gave the elders a chance to teach the gospel to the family they were living with. A goodly number of Latin-American Saints were brought into the Church in this way.

The missionaries had been living with a particular family for about six months, and they were still not interested in hearing about the gospel. They were too hardhearted and set in the ways of the world to be touched by the Spirit and by the gospel truths we tried to teach them. We were convinced that the elders could have continued to live with them for another six months, or even six years, without converting them to the gospel. To make matters worse, the food was poor, and consequently my companion and I were somewhat sick much of the time.

There was no question about it—it was time to find a new home. But where? We didn't want just a roof over our heads—

we were missionaries and had special needs that had to be met if we were going to perform our labors in a manner pleasing to our Heavenly Father. My companion and I decided that our new home had to meet the following requirements:

1. We wanted to live with a family that would be willing to listen to our discussions on the gospel and become members of the Church.
2. We needed good food.
3. We needed a telephone—something that does not exist in every Latin-American home.
4. For transportation convenience, we wanted to live within a four-block area that was close to the center of our district and near several bus lines.

How were we going to find such a home? It would be difficult, so we decided to do the only right thing to do—fast and pray and take the problem to our Heavenly Father for his guidance and direction. We began fasting, and after having prayed to the Lord and told him of our need for a new place to live that would meet those four qualifications if we were to be effective in doing his work, we started to look for our new home.

After a full day of doing everything we could think of, we had, it seemed, nothing to show for our labors. Our faith began to waver.

We had started home with heavy hearts, when my companion and I decided to make one last inquiry of the shopkeeper in the little store we had just passed. The store was in the bottom of a three-story house, the owner having turned her basement into a little store to make some extra money. We were hoping that she would know of someone in the area who rented rooms.

When we asked about a room, the lady mentioned that her aunt might be able to help us out, and she would be willing to inquire for us if we would return the following morning. We went back the next morning just before the end of our fast to ask how it had gone with her aunt.

"Well," she said, "as a matter of fact, I didn't really think my aunt would give you a place, but I wanted to have time to talk to my husband. You see, when you talked to me, the strangest feeling came over me. I asked myself how I would feel if my sons were in America and were looking for a place to live and to eat. I felt such motherly feelings for you that I *had* to find a place for you."

When she had suggested to her husband that they take two young American missionaries into their home, his answer was, "No! I don't want any *gringos* in my house! Besides that, they're not Catholics. I won't have them!"

Well, the Spirit of the Lord had so touched this good lady that she wouldn't take no for an answer, and she kept him up all night until the answer was yes. By the time we arrived she had doubled her children up to make a room available, and everything was "just so."

They were just beautiful people. They had a phone, the lady prepared wonderful food, the house was in the right area, and, to the best of my knowledge, everyone in the family has been baptized except the father, and he seems to be warming up to the idea.

I've thought many times since that experience that the Lord is more than willing to guide us if we will but tune our spiritual ears to his voice, and listen.

THE YEAR OF GREAT FAITH
Elder Matthew Cowley

In March, 1881, a convention was called of representative natives of the Ngatikahungunu Tribe of the Maori race for the purpose of discussing political, social and religious problems of racial importance.

Many of those in attendance were old enough to have seen the coming of the first Christian missionaries to New Zealand, and all were devout adherents to one of the several churches which had already been established among them.

The great native leaders assembled at this convention could conceive of nothing of more vital importance to the well-being of the race than to know the answer to the questions: "Which is *the* church? Which one should the Maori join so there will be once again a unity of religious belief among them? Where was the power of God unto salvation for the Maori race?"

At last it was moved, and the motion approved, that the all-important question should be propounded to one Paora Potangaroa, the wisest chief and most learned sage among them.

Potangaroa's answer was one word, *taihoa,* which means "wait," or "wait awhile," and which, in this instance, implied that he would answer the question later after he had given the matter serious consideration. The old sage then left the assembly and retired to his own residence, which was nearby. There for three days he was occupied in prayer, fasting, and meditation about the problem which had been presented for his solution. He was aware that the true answer would not come without prayerful meditation and without invoking divine aid. After having been thus engaged for three days, he turned to the convention and addressed his people.

Freely translated, these were his words: "My friends, the church for the Maori people has not yet come among us. You will recognize it when it comes. Its missionaries will travel in pairs. They will come from the rising sun. They will visit in our homes. They will learn our language and teach us the gospel in our own tongue. When they pray, they will raise their right hands."

After saying these things, he called Ranginui Kingi to act as scribe [and dictated the following covenants:]

"First, this is the day of the fulness (1881)." Later in that year the LDS missionaries did come to this people, [traveling in pairs and teaching the gospel in their own language].

"Second, the year 1881," he said, "would be the year of the 'sealing' (or the year they would learn of the sealing ordinance).

"Third, the year 1883 will be the year of 'the honoring'— of 'great faith.' " The year 1883 was a year of great honor and great faith among the people of Ngatikahungunu, the tribe of the sage and chief, Potangaroa. Members of this tribe joined the Church of Jesus Christ in great numbers. Members of other tribes of the race also joined the Church in considerable numbers during the same year.

Missionaries had been doing work among the people in New Zealand prior to 1881 but only, with one or two exceptions, among the Europeans. It was in 1881, the year Patangaroa said "the fulness" would come, that Elder W. M. Bromley of Springville, Utah, arrived in New Zealand to preside over the mission, and he was told before leaving home "that the time had come to take the gospel to the Maori people."

A photographer doing business in Masterton in 1881, having heard of the prophecies of Potangaroa . . . asked the natives for permission to photograph it. Permission was granted, and thus a true copy of the "covenant" was preserved. It had been in the possession of one family down through the years and concealed from public view as a sacred document until it was presented to Brother Nopera in 1944. It is now in the possession of the writer.

Potangaroa was only one of several native prophets who foretold the coming of the L.D.S. missionaries to the Maori people.

> Matthew Cowley, "Maori Chief Predicts Coming of LDS Missionaries," *Improvement Era,* September 1950.

MAY I TELL YOU A STORY?
Nadine W. Larson

In August 1958, a whole new world opened to George and Lucy Bloomfield. They were called to serve full-time in the Southwest Indian Mission. The field was white ready to harvest, and Elder and Sister Bloomfield were privileged to "thrust in [their] sickle with [their] might" (D&C 6:3) and taste some of the first fruits, more choice than any they had heretofore tasted.

When President Stephen L Richards set Brother Bloomfield apart, he made a prophetic statement, "Brother Bloomfield, you will spend the remainder of your years in preaching the gospel to the Lamanites." This was exciting news to Brother George, who by this time was thoroughly converted to the cause of the Lamanite.

With hearts full of enthusiasm and strong faith in God, they set out with determination in their first area—Moencopi, Arizona. Moencopi is a village of Hopi Indians in the middle of the Navajo reservation. It is set among the red sand hills like a green oasis, with its watermelons, corn, and trees sprouting up from the bottoms and sides of dried-up washes.

Because the Bloomfields had been warned that Moencopi was a difficult area for proselyting, they were fearful as they began their labors among the Hopi tribe. Nevertheless, nothing can compare to the zeal of new missionaries, and the zeal of this devoted couple was no exception. With prayerful hearts and a determination to succeed, they began to go from door to door to solicit cottage meetings.

The Hopis are typically a friendly people, happy to welcome these white people into their homes for a pleasant visit. After Elder and Sister Bloomfield sat and chatted for awhile with them, they requested time for a meeting. Suddenly the friendliness of the Hopi people was gone. They were "too busy." They had time to be friends with the white man and woman but no time to learn their religion.

With dampened spirits, the Bloomfields returned day after day—with the same results. A month or so passed, and they began to meet with Navajo camps from the surrounding area. They felt comfortable around the Navajos, for it was with this tribe that they had had so much experience. Although they enjoyed working with the Navajos, they realized that their calling was to labor with the Hopis. However, no matter how hard they tried, they could not seem to find a way to break down the resistance in this tightly knit community.

They decided to go to the leader of the community, the governor. When they arrived at Governor Numkena's house, his wife informed them that he was working on his farm in Tuba City, three miles away. A little fearfully, but with a prayer on their lips, they drove down to the farm. Governor Numkena was irrigating his corn. As Elder and Sister Bloomfield got out of their car and walked toward him, he leaned on his shovel and spoke to them. When the missionaries stated their cause, he was polite and friendly, yet he said, "No, do not bother my people. They are too busy."

With sagging hearts, George and Lucy returned to their car and slowly drove home. However, their determination to succeed in the Lord's work soon rallied them, and they began to fast and pray. In the depths of humility, they prayed as they had never prayed before. After two weeks of intensive supplication to the Lord for his intervention, George announced to Lucy that he was going to talk to the governor again. He found the governor once more in his field. This time he was pulling beans on the far side of his bean patch. Without a word, Elder Bloomfield began pulling beans on the opposite side. They worked until they finally met in the middle of the patch, not a word having been spoken. The governor began to pile the beans on his wagon, so Brother George did the same. When the wagon was loaded and the little mule team was hitched up, Governor Numkena told George, "Get up on the seat."

Dusk had fallen as the two men rode along silently on the sandy, rough road. The old mules could not be hurried. At last the Hopi began to speak. "Would you like me to tell you a story as we go along?" he asked.

"Of course," answered George.

The governor launched on a long, detailed history of Moencopi. When he finished, he queried, "Now, isn't that a good story?" The missionary replied, "Yes, it was a good story. Now, may I tell you a story?"

When the governor agreed to this, Brother Bloomfield, with a rapidly beating heart, carefully began to unfold the beautiful story of the Book of Mormon. The Spirit of the Lord bore down heavily upon him as he quietly and sincerely testified that the Indians were descendants of the Book of Mormon people. He bore a fearless testimony to the governor that he knew the Book of Mormon is true and that the governor and his people would be blessed if they listened to the missionaries. As he ended his testimony, the wagon stopped in front of the governor's house. The elder turned to his Hopi companion with the question, "Governor, are you going to let us tell your people about their book and the gospel?"

The reply was, "Go ahead, the doors are open to you."

What could it be called? Moccasin telegraph, perhaps, but whatever it was, the next morning when these humble missionaries returned to their labors, every door was open to them; and by evening they had made many appointments. By the time a busy month had passed, this couple had more work than they could do. They requested help from the mission president, who sent two elders to help take care of the great increase in investigators.

Out of this village came some lovely converts, people who were to add spiritual strength to their community. In Moencopi today there stands a lovely little LDS chapel in which meets an active branch of Lamanites, both Hopis and Navajos, as a living testimony to the faithfulness of George and Lucy Bloomfield.

Nadine W. Larson, "Listen to the Song of Israel," *Improvement Era,* August 1964, p. 686.

PROMPTED TO FAST

Mark Nixon

While on my mission, I had some beautiful experiences from having tapped the power of prayer when combined with fasting. As a missionary, I resorted to fasting for guidance in searching out the honest in heart that would accept the gospel, or when I had an investigator that was in need of the elders' faith and prayers to help him gain a testimony.

For some reason that I could not explain, on one particular day I felt a desire to fast for my younger brother Robert, who was serving in the England Central Mission. There wasn't a concrete reason I could cite why I should fast for him—I just felt as though he needed my faith and prayers in his behalf.

Robert was constantly in my thoughts and silent prayers that day as I went about my own duties as a missionary. That evening, I broke my fast and again asked the Lord for his blessings and protective care to be with Robert. A calm, peaceful feeling came over me and then I knew that all was well with my brother.

It was not until the correspondence of several letters that I learned why I had felt the need to fast for Robert on that particular day. I was amazed to find that on the exact day of my fast Robert and his companion were tracting when they encountered a lady who was possessed by an evil spirit. This can be a terrifying and dangerous experience for even seasoned members of the Church, much less newly ordained young elders. However, through the inspiration of the Lord and the power of the priesthood, they were able to successfully cast out that unclean spirit.

The Lord knew that on this day Robert would be in need of greater faith and spiritual strength than was normally required of him, and somehow this was communicated to me by the Spirit. And even though I was thousands of miles away in the Southern States Mission, through fasting and prayer I was able to sustain and support him in his encounter with that evil spirit. It is possible to appreciate how significant a contribution fasting can be when we read about the disciples' unsuccessful attempts to cast out an evil spirit. Jesus then cast out the evil spirit, instructing his followers that "this kind can come forth by nothing, but by prayer *and fasting."* (Mark 9:29. Italics added.)

Through this and other experiences I have gained a strong testimony of the power of fasting—a power that prepares us to receive the blessings of heaven.

THE LORD'S CABLEGRAM

Elder Matthew Cowley

I know that God lives, I know that Jesus is the Christ, and I know that Joseph Smith was a prophet of the living God. I know that there is inspiration in this Church, and I could talk to you for hours about that. This Church is guided by inspiration. I have had inspiration. I have had come into my heart when I have been officiating in this Church in various capacities inspiration which I did not know I was going to receive and which has solved my problems.

I was lying in bed in Sydney, Australia, worried to death. I had been fasting and praying. We had an enormous problem in one of those missions. I didn't know but what within a few weeks the whole mission would be closed up. All of a sudden, there flashed in my mind the words of a cablegram, and I got dressed and couldn't wait for the post office to open so that I could send that cablegram, and I went and sent it word for word just as I had seen those words flash into my mind in a vision while I was awake. That cablegram solved the whole problem.

Live close to God, brethren in the priesthood. Magnify your callings. He is very close. He wants to use you. Let him use you for the building up of his kingdom.

Address delivered at Portland Stake Conference, March 1952.

GENEALOGY

We have a work to do just as important in its sphere as the Savior's work was in its sphere. Our fathers cannot be made perfect without us; we cannot be made perfect without them. They have done their work and now sleep. We are now called upon to do ours, which is to be the greatest work man ever performed on the earth.

—Brigham Young, *Journal of Discourses,* 18:213

THE LORD "READS" A RECORD
Joan Lloyd Hofheins

My mother's family, the Edward Ashton family, has always been mindful of their obligation to seek out the records of our departed kindred. My early adult years had been filled with the time-consuming demands of raising a large family of my own, so it was not until the last few years that I started to assume my share of the responsibility for doing our family genealogy.

I was given the assignment of reading the microfilms of a parish register from Wales that was recorded in the early 1600s. The original register was written in Old English script and Latin, which is difficult to read in a perfectly preserved record. This particular register, however, was in exceptionally poor condition, with many of the pages being well worn and parts of the record so blurred as to make it almost illegible.

My aunt had told me that we had about ten to twelve family lines that had been recorded in this particular parish register. She stated that I would find the names of a great many of our ancestors on those rolls of film, which were so numerous that it would take a year or more to read all of them. I was instructed that every name that was one of our family surnames would be a relative, and when we had recorded their genealogical information, the temple work could be done for these people, thereby bringing the blessings of the gospel ordinances to a great number of our departed kindred.

I greatly felt my responsibility to those that had gone before me, but the task of completing this time-consuming record and also meeting the daily needs of my family seemed to be almost impossible, though I had the assurance that I would be able to do the work for these ancestors if I were prayerful and had the Spirit of the Lord with me. Thus, it was with a great measure of enthusiasm and confidence that I went to the reading room at the BYU library and proceeded to put the microfilm on the reading machine. I adjusted the machine to bring the film into sharp focus and was shocked to find that the film was not one bit more readable when it was in focus than when it was out of focus. The Old English script looked like a foreign language to me and could not have been more difficult for me to decipher had it actually been a foreign language. I was overwhelmed with the impossibility of my being able to read that record, and quickly came to the conclusion that I was either going to have to have special training in reading English script and Latin, or I would have to get someone else to read the film for me.

I sat for a few moments, disappointed and dejected at having failed to accomplish my assignment. I had not been able to read even one name on the film. And then, as I sat and contemplated what my purpose was in trying to read the film, I realized that I had given up very quickly, without having done everything I possibly could to read the record. There was one thing more I could do, and that was to pray. So I bowed my head and said a short prayer and asked the Lord to please help me to understand the Old English script and to be able to read the names of my ancestors that were recorded on that roll of film.

I then decided to try to read the film once more. The first page of the register was so poorly preserved that I felt that it would be impossible to ever read any of the names on that page, even if I mastered the art of reading Old English script. I decided that I would turn the film forward to another page that was more legible when I received the distinct impression that some of the people listed on that page had been waiting longer to have their temple work done than those whose names would appear in more recent and readable records. I also received a very strong impression that they were just as important as anyone else whose name would appear later in those records, and needed their work done as much as did the others, if not more.

As I continued to look at the strange penmanship on that page, a miracle began to take place! Certain names gradually became very clear and I could easily read them and determine that they were my ancestors. I read on and was able to decipher the dates of birth, baptism, and deaths of those who had our family surnames. After I recorded this information and turned the viewer to the next page of the register, *all* of the handwriting would be illegible. After looking at the page intently for a few moments, another name would suddenly start to clear and I was able to easily read the information on that family member while all the writing surrounding it was totally unreadable. It was a thrilling experience for me as I gratefully recorded many names of my ancestors that day.

I excitedly related the experience to my family that evening, and they were also impressed with the way the Lord had helped me to read the microfilm. My sixteen-year-old daughter Carolyn was especially impressed and touched by this experience and requested that she be given the opportunity to try to read the film. I was delighted at her interest, but felt that I should caution her that it would take more than just a casual interest and curiosity to be able to read the record. I told her that she would have to prepare herself spiritually first, by fasting and prayer. This she willingly did, and excitedly joined me at the library, hoping and praying that she would also be given the blessing of being able to read the record.

It was a very choice and exciting experience for both of us as Carolyn had exactly the same experience of having the Spirit of the Lord help her to read the names of our ancestors. We could feel that guiding influence of his Spirit as we continued to "read" through the films that day. Several times we were prompted to recheck a certain area of the film, only to find that we had missed a name. In our excitement to progress as fast as possible with the work, we had turned the film ahead without waiting sufficiently for the Spirit to assist us in reading the film. This was truly a testimony to me that those people were ready and waiting to have their work done in the temples of the Lord and were there to assist in completing their record.

My fifteen-year-old son Timothy, who has also received a testimony of the work for the redemption of the dead, requested the privilege of assisting with the reading of the microfilms. After a period of fasting and prayer, he too joined us at the library and had the same experiences as we had had in reading the films. The three of us have since spent many enjoyable and rewarding hours reading the films of that parish register and have been able to record the names and dates of more than four hundred of our ancestors.

It has been a very thrilling and gratifying experience for me to share in my children's love for their departed kindred, even to the point where they have encouraged and prodded me in the work of completing our family genealogy. And this experience has also been an unforgettable witness to me that the Lord loves *all* his children and ministers to their needs, even those who are "dead."

IF WE DO ALL WE CAN

Joyce Lindstrom

I knew that the Van Hooser family had settled in Bethany, Missouri, at an early date. I met my cousin Jay Lamb in Columbia, Missouri, and from there we drove to Bethany.

In Bethany we went to the county clerk's office. The only records in that office of genealogical value to us were birth records. While I copied the Van Hooser names from those registers, something kept saying to me, "Go into another room. Don't waste your time here."

When I had copied those records, we went into the room where the marriage and deed records were kept. As I tried to copy the Van Hooser marriages from the records, this same insistent feeling recurred—"Go to another room. Don't waste your time here." Now, as valuable as marriage records are, I couldn't understand this inner urge to quit working in these records. But finally I couldn't concentrate on the marriages, and told Jay that I was going into the probate office.

While working on the Van Hooser probates, I ran across the probate record of Lydia Van Hooser. Reading through her records, I found her to be my Lydia Van Hooser who had lived previously in Troy, Illinois. I knew this branch of the Van Hooser family had left Troy by 1860, when the census was taken, but I didn't know where they had gone.

Now I knew. Since Lydia Van Hooser never married, she had left her property to sisters, nieces, and nephews. This is why I had to go to Bethany—to find this will and all other papers pertaining to the distribution of Lydia's estate. Once I knew this was where the Van Hooser descendants had moved, I searched the probate records regarding our surnames of interest to me, and found a wealth of genealogical information. I worked most of the day in the probate office. When I felt as though I had covered the records there, I returned to the room where the marriages were kept. I was then able to concentrate on the marriages and found a great many more pertaining to those mentioned in Lydia Van Hooser's will than I would ever have found or identified before.

Genealogy is the Lord's work and if we do all we can in behalf of our ancestors and still need more help, the aid of the Lord is always nearby. What we must do is kneel in prayer, with faith, and ask for divine aid.

Improvement Era, September 1964.

INFORMATION FROM THE LORD
K. Haybron Adams

In my late teens I became a member of the Church—the only member of my family to do so. Thus, I alone bear the responsibility of searching out the records for the departed members of my family and doing the temple work for them. Perhaps this explains why the spirit of Elijah has rested so heavily upon me.

My father's family, the Howards, were very prominent members of the community in Zanesville, Ohio, which is some distance from my former residence in Denver, Colorado. I therefore attempted to obtain the information I needed by mail. I had written the caretaker of the Zanesville cemetery requesting information on death dates that could be obtained from tombstones in the Howard family lot, if the family members in question had been buried there. It was essential that I ascertain these death dates, for at that time family group sheets would not be accepted for temple work unless all of the information was complete—including the death date.

Since I never received a reply to that letter, nor had my check been cashed, I decided that the best approach would be to go to the Zanesville cemetery and check the records and tombstones personally.

After arriving at the Zanesville cemetery, I went to the caretaker's house where I was given permission to examine the records. Upon opening one of the books, I found my letter and the check! I surmise that when they received my letter they started looking for the information I had requested, but something had interrupted them. The book was then closed on the letter, which they were unable to find again.

I put the check in my pocket, and resumed my search for information on the Adams and Howard families. I recorded the information I needed on the Adams line from the books in the caretaker's office, and then requested information on the lot designation for the Howard family, which I was given along with a map.

I first visited Grandmother Adams's grave and from there I drove to the Howard lot. I parked the car next to an overflowing lilac bush that almost obscured a large pink granite tombstone on the lot that the map indicated as adjoining the Howard lot. I then left the car and walked the few steps to the Howard family lot—a large grassy lot partially shaded by a grouping of maple trees to the left.

The markers, all of which were of grey granite approximately fifteen inches high, were identical, something not usually seen in a family lot with dates going back to 1785. Upon examining these markers, to my great delight I found the names I had been searching for—Rachel Julia Howard, her brothers and sister: George Gist Howard, Caroline Howard, Joseph W. Howard and his wife, Mary E. Howard—and many generations of Howards for whom I had no record.

I eagerly began copying the information from each of these grey tombstones into my brown record book. I then had the information that I needed to complete my family group sheets, and more. The trip had been worthwhile and successful.

As it was late in the afternoon and the cemetery was due to close at five o'clock, I hurried on to another section and was able to again record valuable names and dates in my brown book. Having recorded all the information available on my lines before closing time, I decided to return to the Howard lot to take a picture for my father, who has a great love and interest in his family history.

I drove back to the middle of the cemetery where the Howard lot was located, but I was unable to find the lot with the grey tombstones. The caretaker's cottage was nearby, so I returned and again asked for directions to the Howard lot. He checked the coordinates, the record designating the location of the burial lots, and found the listing for the Howard family.

Following the caretaker's directions, I drove back to the Howard family lot, this time driving past that profuse lilac bush and parking directly in front of the family lot. The maple trees were there on my left, but there was not a tombstone in the whole lot—not one! Just grass! I was standing where I had stood before while copying down names and dates into my brown book, but now there was nothing to copy or photograph. I was completely mystified—I couldn't figure it out!

As I stood there wondering about this unexplainable situation, I began to realize that it was time for the cemetery to close. I ceased my puzzling and proceeded to drive to a relative's home, as I did not wish to spend the night in the cemetery.

Almost immediately after I arrived home I began verifying the names and dates that I had recorded while in the cemetery, and all of the information was correct—including the data taken from those grey tombstones on the Howard lot! I was delighted, but still mystified as to why the tombstones were not visible when I returned to the lot the second and third times.

And then, slowly but surely it began to dawn on me exactly what had occurred—something I cannot explain physically or logically—only spiritually. The tombstones were there and remained so until I had copied the necessary information, and then everything reverted to the condition it had been originally, and as it now is. I can explain this only by assuming that these ancestors must have accepted the gospel and the Lord assisted them in making known the information that was necessary to perform their temple work.

A rational and logical analysis would dictate that those grey tombstones were an offspring of an illusionary mind, were it not for the names and dates written in a little brown book which I still have in my possession.

KEYS ARE NOT LEFT IN CHURCH DOORS
Jack Jarrard

A note from the Thomas Henry Clark family organization in Grantsville, Utah, reports a very unusual story in their search for information on a certain family member. The family was having difficulties working each parish and county library in England, so they had a special day for fasting and prayer. The note says:

"Researchers were able to keep an appointment at Withington parish, but were disappointed in not finding the particular information for Rebecca Carwardine Probert—wife of Thomas Probert, clerk of Holy Orders. They had been informed by the family group that Rebecca's mother was born at Preston Wynn, two miles from Withington. The roads weren't too good and there was difficulty in finding the church—in fact, they wound up finding the church in the middle of a cow pasture and found an old brass key in the door. To their surprise it did unlock the door, and they checked the pews for family names—the first was Rebecca's family—John Carwardine. Other records of the family were noted on plaques.

"The church seemed to be still in use, so researchers tried to find the vicar so records could be searched. They stumbled upon an old metal box by the door. They lifted the lid and peered in, and on top of the papers was the marriage certificate for Thomas Probert, clerk of Holy Orders, and Rebecca Carwardine.

"This ended a twenty-year search for the certificate. Researchers reminded the family that keys are not left in church doors, nor parish records left on the floor by the doors, as a general rule."

"A Genealogical Story," *Church News,* December 7, 1968, p. 8.

YOUR PROGENITORS WILL BE PLEASED

Peter E. Johnson

I was called on a mission to the Southern States in the spring of 1898. I reached Mississippi the twenty-second of June, 1898. On the eighth of August I was taken down with the chills and fever, which turned to malaria. I became so low that the president sent his counselor and two elders to see me in relation to being released and sent home. The yellow fever quarantine came on; I was not able to leave; and then I had the following experience:

I was lying on a bed, burning up with fever, and the elders who had been sent to ascertain my condition were very much alarmed. They stepped out of the room and held whispered consultations. They were so far away that under ordinary conditions I could not have heard what was said; but in some manner my hearing was made so keen that I heard their conversation as well as if they had been at my bedside. They said it was impossible to think of my recovering, and that I never would go home unless I went in a box. They therefore decided they might just as well notify the president and make necessary arrangements.

The following day I asked to be removed into the hall, where it was cooler. I was lying on a pallet (or bed). There was an attendant with me, the others having gone to Sunday School, which was being held about one hundred yards away. Soon after they had left, I was apparently in a dying condition, and my attendant became so fearful of my appearance and condition that he left me. I desired a drink of water but of course was unable to get it myself. I became discouraged, and wondered why it was that I was sent to Mississippi and whether it was simply to die in the field. I felt that I would prefer death, rather than live and endure the fever and the agony through which I was passing. I thought of my people at home and of the conditions then surrounding me, and decided that I might just as well pass from this life. Just as I reached that conclusion, this thought came to me: "You will not die unless you choose death." This was a new thought, and I hesitated to consider the question; then I made the choice that I would rather die.

Soon after that, my spirit left the body; just how I cannot tell, but I perceived myself standing some four or five feet in the air, and saw my body lying on the bed. I felt perfectly natural, but as this was a new condition, I began to make observations. I turned my head, shrugged my shoulders, felt with my hands, and realized that it was myself. I also knew that my body was lying lifeless on the bed. While I was in a new environment, it did not seem strange, for I realized everything that was going on, and perceived that I was the same in the spirit as I had been in the body. While contemplating this new condition, something attracted my attention, and on turning around I beheld a personage, who said, "You did not know that I was here." I replied, "No, but I see you are. Who are you?" "I am your guardian angel; I have been following you constantly while on earth." I asked, "What will you do now?" He replied, "I am to report your presence, and you will remain here until I return." He informed me, on returning, that we should wait there, as my sister desired to see me, but was busy just at that time. Presently she came. She was glad to see me and asked if I was offended because she kept me waiting. She explained that she was doing some work that she wished to finish.

Just before my eldest sister died she asked me to enter into this agreement: That if she died first, she was to watch over me, protect me from those who might seek my downfall, and that she would be the first to meet me after death. If I happened to die first, she wished me to do the same for her. We made this agreement, and this was the reason that my sister was the first one of my relatives to meet me. After she arrived, my mother and other sisters and friends came to see me and we discussed various topics, as we would do here on meeting friends. After we had spent some little time in conversation, the guide came to me with a message that I was wanted by some of the apostles who had lived on the earth in this dispensation.

As soon as I came into their presence, I was asked if I desired to remain there. This seemed strange, for it had never occurred to me that we would have any choice there in the spirit world as to whether we should remain or return to the earth life. I was asked if I felt satisfied with conditions there. I informed them that I was, and had no desire to return to the fever and misery from which I had been suffering while in the body. After some little conversation this question was repeated with the same answer. Then I asked, "If I remain, what will I be asked to do?" I was informed that I would preach the gospel to the spirits there, as I had been preaching it to the people here, and that I would do so under the immediate direction of the Prophet Joseph. This remark brought to my mind a question which has been much discussed here, as to whether or not the Prophet Joseph is now a resurrected being. While I did not ask the question, they read it in my mind, and immediately said, "You wish to know whether the Prophet has his body or not?" I replied, "Yes, I would like to know." I was told that the Prophet Joseph Smith has his body, as also his brother Hyrum, and that as soon as I could do more with my body than I could do without it, my body would be resurrected.

I was again asked if I desired to remain. This bothered me considerably, for I had already expressed myself as being satisfied. I then inquired why it was that I was asked so often if I was satisfied and if I desired to remain. I was then informed that my progenitors had made a request that if I chose, I might be granted the privilege of returning to again take up my mortal body, in order that I might gather my father's genealogy and do the necessary work in the temple for my ancestors. As I was still undecided, one of the apostles said, "We will now show you what will take place if you remain here in the spirit world, after which you can decide."

When we returned to the place where my body was lying, I was informed with emphasis that my first duty would be to watch the body until after it had been disposed of, as that was necessary knowledge for me to have in the resurrection. I then saw the elders send a message to President Rich, at Chattanooga, and in due time all preparations were made for the shipment of my body to Utah. One thing seemed peculiar to me, that I was able to read the telegram as it ran along the wires, as easily as I could read the pages of a book. I could see President Rich when he received the telegram in Chattanooga. He walked the floor, wringing his hands, with the thought in his mind, "How can I send a message to his father?"

The message was finally sent, and I could follow it on the wire. I saw the station and the telegraph operator at Price, Utah. I heard the instrument click as the message was received, and saw the operator write out the message and send it by phone from Price to Huntington. I also saw clearly the Huntington office and the man who received the message. I could see clearly and distinctly the people on the street. I did not have to hear what was said, for I was able to read their thoughts from their countenances. The message was delivered to my aunt, who went out with others to find my father. In due time he received the message. He did not seem to be overcome by the news, but began to make preparations to meet the body.

I then saw my father at the railroad station in Price, waiting for my body to arrive. Apparently he was unaffected, but when he heard the whistle of the train which was carrying my body, he went behind the depot and cried as if his heart would break. While I had been accompanying the body en route, I was still able to see what was going on at home. The distance apparently did not affect my vision. As the train approached the station, I went to my father's side and, seeing his great anguish, I informed my companion that I would return. He expressed his approval of my decision and said he was pleased with the choice I had made.

By some spiritual power, all these things had been shown to me as they would occur if I did not return to the body. Immediately upon making this choice or decision, my companion said, "Good. Your progenitors will be pleased with your decision." I asked the question why, and I was told that it was their desire that I should return to the body, hunt up my father's genealogies, and do their work in the temple. . . .

Just how my spirit entered the body I cannot tell, but I saw the apostle place his hands upon the head of my prostrate body, and almost instantly I realized that the change had come and I was again in the body. The first thing that I knew, I felt a warm life-giving spot on the crown of my head, which passed through my entire body, going out to the tips of my fingers and toes. I then heard distinctly the same words that had been pronounced by Elder Grant when I was set apart for my mission, "Go in peace and return in safety." After entering the body, I saw no more of the messengers who had been accompanying me, but I had a vivid recollection of all that had taken place.

Relief Society Magazine, August 1920, pp. 449-455.

HEALINGS

I can bear testimony that the sick have been healed, the blind have been made to see, the deaf to hear, and the lame to walk, and devils have been cast out, by the power of God. These gifts and graces have been with this people from the organization of the Church until the present hour.

—Wilford Woodruff, *Deseret Weekly News,*
38:451, March 5, 1889

USE YOUR PRIESTHOOD
Steve Taylor

While serving in the Andes South Mission, I was assigned to work in Oruro, Bolivia. Oruro is a mining town of about 85,000 people, at an altitude of 13,500 feet.

The first few days I spent in Oruro's altitude were difficult and trying. It was difficult just to get enough oxygen to breathe, and there was a constant headache to contend with due to the rapid and dramatic change in altitude from my previous assignment. But, like all the other missionaries that had gone before me, I adjusted to the altitude within a few days and was soon attacking my missionary labors with enthusiasm and vigor.

Several months later I received a telegram telling me that my new companion, Elder Seegmiller, would be arriving on Thursday. I met him at the train station and then we took a taxi to our apartment. By the time we arrived, Elder Seegmiller was breathing very hard, but that was normal, so I wasn't concerned about it.

We unpacked his bags and went out to work. We joked about the thin air, neither of us taking his shortness of breath too seriously.

We had a cottage meeting that night which was within walking distance of our apartment. Elder Seegmiller had a difficult time just walking to the meeting, and when we returned home about 10:30, he complained that he was quite tired and immediately went to bed.

The next morning when the alarm went off at six o'clock, I popped out of bed and said, "O.K. Let's get going!"

I heard some groans from the other bed and then, "I'm sick!"

I thought to myself that either his body was still adjusting to the altitude, or he was one of those elders who had a hard time getting up at six o'clock in the morning. I said, "Let's have prayer and we'll see what happens."

We had our prayer. He said he was still sick, so he went back to sleep while I studied for a while. When it was time to go out, I got him back up and we went out and worked until noon. He was really breathing hard all morning. He told me that as a youngster in California he had had problems with his heart, a rheumatic condition, I believe. When his doctor found out that he had been called on a mission to Bolivia, the doctor told him that he couldn't go because of the extreme altitude of much of the country. Elder Seegmiller did some research on the mission and found that some parts of the mission are down in the jungle at very low altitudes. The doctor then gave permission for him to go to Bolivia, but made it very clear that he would have to stay at the lower altitudes in the mission.

When Elder Seegmiller arrived in the mission field, he was assigned to one of the jungle areas. When he was reassigned to Oruro, he hesitated to remind the mission president of his heart condition and accepted his new assignment with the conviction that since he was doing the Lord's work, the Lord would take care of him.

By that afternoon Elder Seegmiller wasn't feeling too well and he chose to remain in bed rather than to go out tracting. So I took a local companion and went on with the work.

The next morning when six o'clock came, my request that we get out of bed was again answered by grumbles and groans. Again I said, "Let's have prayer and see what happens." We had prayer, and Elder Seegmiller went back to bed.

I worked with a local companion all morning and when I came back at noon Elder Seegmiller was really breathing hard. Because he kept getting worse instead of better, I began to doubt that his body was ever going to adjust.

I spent the afternoon tracting, returning to the apartment house about four o'clock that afternoon. The landlord was there and began berating me for having left my companion when he was so terribly sick. We went in to our room and I could hardly believe the condition he was in! All of the color was gone from his face and he was gasping for air.

He needed a doctor, and fast. We went out trying to locate a doctor, but there aren't many doctors in their offices on a Saturday afternoon in Bolivia. We couldn't find a doctor anywhere, so we decided to go back to the apartment and do the best that we could for Elder Seegmiller when the landlord saw one of the doctors we had been looking for walking along the street on his way home. He was the one and only heart specialist in the city, and were we ever glad to see him!

He examined Elder Seegmiller and stated excitedly, "He's going to die if he isn't taken out of this altitude right now!"

But there was no way to get him out of Oruro. The only transportation out of that city was a plane that comes in once a week, and the train. The train went out each morning, but in order to get a ticket you had to have a reservation at least three weeks in advance.

"Doctor, you've got to help him hold on until morning, and then we'll get him on that train somehow," I said.

The doctor gave him some shots and gave me some drops to give him orally that would dilate his veins and arteries. And, following the doctor's instructions, I went to the pharmacy to get some oxygen. They had one large, balloon-type bag which they filled with oxygen. I rented the bag, ran back to the apartment and inserted the attached nozzle in Elder Seegmiller's mouth.

He seemed to be breathing a little easier, so I left and called the mission home by short-wave radio and informed them of Elder Seegmiller's condition and probable arrival in the morning. I then returned to the apartment, packed Elder Seegmiller's belongings, and began a night of worrying and praying. Every ten minutes or so I would get down on my knees and say a short prayer, then begin worrying again. I became even more worried as I watched his color change to a grayish color.

About two o'clock in the morning, I realized that there wasn't enough oxygen to last him through the night. About four-fifths of the oxygen was gone, and he still had about half the night to go. I explained that I was going to take the oxygen bag to the pharmacy to have it filled again, but he gave no indication that he understood what I was saying.

I took the oxygen bag and ran as fast as I could to the pharmacy. I pounded on the door and awakened the pharmacist, who filled it as quickly as he could, and then I dashed back to the apartment.

I just about collapsed when I looked at Elder Seegmiller. He was actually blue! I ran over and thrust the oxygen bag nozzle in his mouth. Then I noticed that he wasn't breathing. I panicked and started shaking him and yelling at him to start breathing, which didn't help at all. Hysterically, I threw up my hands and said, "What on earth do I do now?"

As I did that, a message came to me just as clear and strong as anything has ever come to me in my life. It said, "Use your priesthood."

And I thought to myself, "Of course! Why didn't I think of that?"

I immediately laid my hands on Elder Seegmiller's head and through the priesthood commanded him to start breathing again. As soon as I did that, he began breathing.

I heaved one tremendous sigh of relief. It didn't take long to kneel down and thank the Lord for the inspiration that was given me in my time of extreme need, and, most of all, for the power of the holy priesthood that I held.

The rest of the night was hard, but at least Elder Seegmiller was breathing and there was more than enough oxygen for him. Morning finally came.

The president of the branch in Oruro worked at the train station and had been informed about Elder Seegmiller's difficulties, so he was at the train station earlier than usual that Sunday morning, trying to get two tickets for Elder Seegmiller and me. But, of course, they had been sold out for a long time, so he wasn't able to get any tickets.

Elder Seegmiller *had* to leave on that train, even if he didn't have a ticket that entitled him to a seat, so I took him to the station and tried to make arrangements to have him lie in the aisle. Due to certain regulations and safety factors, the train official refused to allow it.

I didn't know what we were going to do, but ten minutes before the train was due to leave, a man approached a group of people standing nearby and said, "I won't be using this ticket. Would anyone like to buy it?"

I literally grabbed the ticket out of his hand before anyone else had the chance to indicate that they might want it. Now Elder Seegmiller had his seat on the train, but he was still unconscious and needed someone to give him his drops and make sure that the oxygen nozzle remained in his mouth. I couldn't find anyone taking that train who was willing to take that responsibility.

Then, about three minutes before the train was due to leave, another man announced to the crowd, "I have a ticket for today's train. Does anyone want to buy it?"

I ran over to him and quickly purchased the ticket. Much to my surprise, I found that this ticket was for a seat right next to the other one!

I had only enough time to place Elder Seegmiller in his seat and check to make sure that he was getting enough oxygen before the train pulled out of the station. Remembering that the train would be climbing to an even higher elevation over the pass before we would be descending to the jungle lowlands, I gave Elder Seegmiller his drops, plus a few more, to help him at the higher altitude. He made it over the pass without too much more difficulty in breathing, perhaps in spite of my overdose of medication. As we began our descent, the color began to return to his face and he regained consciousness. By the time we reached the valley he was feeling quite well, except for a few hunger pangs.

This was an experience I shall never forget. I learned that the Lord truly is watching over his missionaries and protecting them, just as he is always there to bless each of us in our times of need. Most important, I learned that his power (the priesthood) is real and can work miracles. I know, because I've seen it happen.

A COMMAND TO HEAL

Douglas G. Cannon

As returned missionaries, Frank Kirton and I had the opportunity of living in the Delta Phi fraternity house in Salt Lake City while we worked and went to school. The young men that lived there were often called on to go to the University Hospital and administer to the sick.

One evening as we were having dinner, one of the young doctors from the hospital, who was also a past member of the same fraternity, came to the house. He told us that one of his patients had leukemia and was not expected to live more than a day or two. The drugs they had been administering to her were no longer effective in controlling the pain, so she was suffering intensely. The patient was of Oriental descent, and a Buddhist by faith, although her husband was a member of the LDS Church. The doctor asked us if we would go to the hospital that evening and administer to her to relieve the pain until she passed away.

That evening we went to the hospital to administer to her. Before we could enter her room, we were required to put on sterilized caps and gowns. We were not prepared for the pitiful sight that greeted us—a little old lady wasted away to skin and bones, with tubes protruding from almost every part of her body. As we looked at her, we felt that death could bring only peace, not sorrow.

We introduced ourselves as elders from her husband's church and told her that we had been asked to give her a blessing. She nodded that she wanted one and indicated that she understood the procedure.

We anointed her with oil, then we laid our hands on her head with the intention of blessing her with relief from pain. As my hands touched her head, I felt impressed—in fact, commanded—to bless her with a complete restoration of health so that she could return home to her family! But the doctor's words, "She's going to die soon," kept going through my mind and I just didn't have enough strength or faith to heal that woman. I finally finished the blessing, but only after blessing her with relief from pain, instead of healing her as I had been commanded.

Afterwards, Frank and I sat in the car and reflected on the experience. He had also felt the witness of the Spirit that the woman was to be healed and that the blessing we had given her was not what the Lord had desired. We decided that we should give her another blessing to restore her health, *after* we had fasted and prayed for the necessary faith.

We went back to the hospital the next evening and were told by one of the nurses that this lady was not expected to live through the night. However, as we placed our hands on her head we again felt the Spirit of the Lord, and this time we were able to bless her with health and strength and told her that she would soon be able to return home and resume her duties as a wife and mother.

We left the hospital that night with the most wonderful feeling, knowing that we had finally done what the Lord wanted us to do.

Several weeks later I was discussing an assignment with a young Japanese girl in my English literature class when she abruptly asked, "Are you a Mormon?"

"Yes," I replied.

"Well," she said, "the strangest thing happened a couple of weeks ago. I'm a nurse at the hospital and was on duty one evening when two rather typical looking college students came in, put on caps and gowns and went into one of my patients' rooms. I noticed them going into the room so I asked another nurse who they were, and she replied, "Mormon elders." We had expected this patient to pass away that night, but when I went in to check on her condition later that evening, I found that she was feeling much better. In fact, she was sitting up in bed. Before the evening was over, we removed all the tubes from her body and she was eating normally again. Within a week, all indications of leukemia had disappeared and she was released to go home! I understand that she is still feeling well and is quite happy. I have been told that the Mormons give blessings and that she may have been given a blessing. Doug, I would give anything to know what power those two young men possessed to be able to heal that woman!"

One of the young men in the fraternity was a stake missionary so we immediately made arrangements for him to give her the missionary lessons. We found out later that the nurse's mother and little sister had joined the Church a few months earlier, but neither she nor her father would listen to the missionary discussions. Both Frank and I moved from the fraternity house a short time later, but the stake missionary has since told us that the nurse and her father were attending church and expected to be baptized within a very short time.

I feel that it was the will of the Lord that this young Japanese nurse witness the effects of the healing power of the priesthood so that she would be more receptive to the gospel. The Lord works in many ways, sometimes by performing a mighty miracle, to bring those spirits into the Church who will faithfully serve him and build up his kingdom.

YOU WILL LIVE TO BE OF SERVICE
Michael Robert Johnson

A good number of young American boys did not return home from the Vietnam conflict as they had left—healthy, strong, and physically able. I was one of them. When I left Vietnam in January of 1968, I left behind my buddies of the 7th Marine Regiment—and both of my legs. I also sustained massive abdominal and head injuries and suffered the loss of one or more fingers on each hand, so I returned, not to the family home in Huntington, West Virginia, but to a veterans hospital in Salt Lake City where I could receive the necessary medical care and surgery that I needed.

My wounds began to heal and my strength began to return enough that the doctors decided that I could withstand corrective surgery. The first of what was to be a seemingly endless series of operations began with surgery to restore as much function as possible to my left hand. What was left of my middle finger was removed so that the remaining fingers could grow closer together and thus be of more use to me. At the same time, a silicone joint was implanted in my ring finger. I remember this hand operation as being one of the most painful surgeries I had to endure. I suppose that is due to the large number of nerve endings that are found in the fingers. The pain was so unbearable that I began asking for pain shots immediately upon coming out of the anesthetic.

The pain continued to be severe the following day. To add to my discomfort, my temperature began to rise rapidly and I began to have trouble focusing on the friends and relatives that had come to my bedside to comfort me. Instead of becoming more lucid as days went by, I became quite groggy and disoriented.

My next contact with reality was two weeks later when I awakened in isolation only to learn that I had been under treatment for hepatitis. Again, things managed to get worse before they got better—jaundice set in. In time, though, I was free from both the pain from the surgery and the discomforts of hepatitis. Before long, I was able to enjoy the simple pleasure of being able to leave my hospital room. I would push my wheelchair through the hospital halls and visit with the other patients.

This period of well-being and freedom from discomfort did not last long. My left hip began to be unusually sensitive and a small sore developed on the front of my hip bone. I wasn't overly concerned, as I assumed it was the result of another piece of shrapnel working its way out, or some old stitches coming to the surface, as had happened many times before.

My temperature began to rise again, which the doctors felt indicated that the hepatitis was returning. However, the next morning I awoke to find that I was lying in a pool of pussy fluid. For the next few days, a thick yellow substance continued to flow from the two holes that had broken open over my hip bone.

Lab tests confirmed that my new affliction was cancer of the bone. The openings began healing and the draining process ceased, which was not desirable, as the enclosed infection was slowly poisoning my system and weakening my body. The only possible way to correct this damaging situation was to surgically reopen the holes so the drainage process would continue until I could gain the necessary strength to undergo the extensive surgery for removal of the malignant bone tissue. My father was informed that I was too weak from my bout with hepatitis to withstand even this relatively minor surgery. Without surgery the doctors felt assured that I would not survive, but neither would I survive the surgery.

Well, my father is a man of great faith. He refused to accept the doctor's decision that I could not possibly live, and asked my cousin Dale to send someone to the hospital who had enough faith in the healing power of the priesthood that he would not be shaken by the doctor's decree that I would die. Not all holders of the Melchizedek Priesthood have that great faith. Dad was certain there was one group of men that possessed the faith to heal the sick, even those afflicted with the deadly disease of cancer. "If at all possible," he instructed Dale, "please have one of the Twelve

Apostles come to the hospital to give Mike a blessing and then I *know* he will live."

We realized that this was not a realistic request, as neither of us had ever had any association with a member of the Quorum of the Twelve. We were hopeful, but did not really expect them to respond to a plea to give a blessing to someone not known to them, especially when the faith and authority to give the blessing I desired is exercised by many men in the Church whose time is not so precious.

My fever reached the point that I again began to lose awareness of my surroundings. I continued to slip in and out of reality as I waited anxiously for Dale to bring someone to administer to me.

Later that evening Dale came to my hospital room and informed me that he had made arrangements for me to have a blessing that would be given by an apostle! I knew then that all was going to be well with me, that if an apostle gave me that blessing, and if it was the Lord's will, I *knew* I would live. I had no doubt—perhaps because I was still young enough that I hadn't lost that trusting childhood faith in the loving care of our Heavenly Father.

I wanted so much to hear and remember every word of that blessing I was to receive at the hands of Elder Gordon B. Hinckley, but that was not possible in my semi-conscious state. Knowing that I would want to have an accurate record of this sacred experience, Dale's wife, Patty, arranged for her sister to be present and record the blessing.

Dale anointed me and then Elder Hinckley gave me a powerful blessing in which he told me that our prayers had been heard, and he promised that I would live to be of service to those about me. Then, in the name of the Lord Jesus Christ, he commanded, "We rebuke this disease, that the healing processes may go forward and clear the infection in your body."

The Spirit was overpowering, but comforting. There were tears of joy as my family and I thanked him—and the Lord—for my blessing and my life. My temperature soon began to subside somewhat. By the next day I was more keenly aware of my surroundings and the treatments I was receiving from the hospital staff. The nurses continued to take samples and run routine lab tests, when the infectious material within me suddenly "exploded" and was expelled from my hip. A new opening above my hip bone continued to drain large amounts of matter for several days.

The doctors and the medical staff were, of course, quite pleased with this unexpected turn of events. Now that my hip had been voluntarily drained of the infectious material, they felt that it would be possible for me to gain the necessary strength to survive the surgical removal of the cancerous bone tissue. The doctors ordered more samples to be taken and tests performed to help determine the extent of the surgery that would be necessary. The lab reports came back indicating that there were no longer any malignant cells in my body. The doctors were dumbfounded and unbelieving then as they are now—more than seven years later—and I am still cancer free!

The doctors have been amazed by my complete recovery, but they shouldn't be, for I was given a blessing by an inspired servant of the Lord who promised me that I would live.

YOU MUST SUFFER WITHOUT MURMURING

[The Colonia Morelos Ward in Sonora, Mexico, was building a tithing granary and Bishop O. P. Brown, with three companions, were pulling up some heavy green timbers to lay across the building for beams to carry the roof of dirt. The scaffold gave way and all fell to the ground. Bishop Brown's own words follow:]

"I fell fourteen feet head-first and as my head struck the ground, a log weighing about five hundred pounds struck me on the hips. My neck was broken, also my right shoulder and elbow, and this log crushed my skull. While I was under this log the impression came to me strongly that I would not die from these injuries. Pablo Sosa removed the log from my body. He straightened up my body and put me on one of the logs. I was conscious of the conditions and asked him to raise my head, which he did. The brethren carried me to the house and administered to me and I told them not to fear, for notwithstanding my critical condition I had a strong impression that I would not die from these injuries.

"They immediately sent for Dr. Keate, who was at a mining camp, and he came four days later. On examining my neck, skull and shoulder, he said my neck was broken and he feared if he tried to adjust the joints under present conditions it might cause my death. So I remained thus, with two joints of my neck out of place, till the present time.

"My shoulder and elbow were adjusted and my skull seemed to have only been cracked. While I was suffering in these conditions I found in my right arm the severest pain that I ever have experienced and it was continued for twenty-four hours until I was left without any physical strength because of the severe pain. It seemed that I could get no relief and that my life was fast ebbing away. In my agony I cried out to the Lord and asked him to relieve this suffering or take me to himself. In that instant there came a voice to me.

"It said, 'My son, if you cannot suffer the things your father suffered, you cannot come where I am. You must suffer without murmuring.' I knew that this was the voice of my earthly father, James Brown, and that he was standing by my side. With this knowledge of my father being at my side and pleading for me and sympathizing for me, tears came into my eyes.

"I said, 'Oh, Father! Forgive me for murmuring and help me to realize and feel the spirit of repentance and relieve me of this suffering by letting thy blessings come to me. And for this knowledge and testimony and the understanding that my earthly father is here with me, I would be willing that my body be torn to pieces, or any other suffering thou seest fit to send me.'

"Immediately I was relieved of all suffering and pain and a blessing came to me that is impossible to express in words, for the Spirit of the Lord was there to the extent that I could not express myself further. . . . And, from that moment on, my strength rapidly grew until I was able in three weeks' time to get into a buggy and come to Juarez to conference over that rough road. A miracle had been wrought, and, as Dr. Keate wrote in *The Scientific Medical Journal,* my case was one in a million that I should live under these circumstances."

N. B. Lundwall, *Faith Like the Ancients* (Salt Lake City: Paragon Printing Company, 1950), pp. 77-79.

HE COULD NOT SEE A MIRACLE EVERY DAY

There was a doctor by the name of Harvey Tate living near to Brother (Martin H.) Peck in Ohio (about 1836), who became somewhat interested in the doctrines of the Latter-day Saints, and for the purpose of learning more concerning them made a visit to his house. While he was there, Brother Peck's son James was brought home with a broken arm, caused by his falling from a tree. The fracture was about three inches above the wrist joint, and so complete that his arm formed a right angle at the place where it was broken. The doctor set and bandaged it, and the boy was put in bed. The pain was so great, however, that he could scarcely endure it, and after the doctor had gone he begged his father to bless him, saying he knew that would cure him.

Brother Peck accordingly administered to him and the pain immediately ceased. He slept well during the night and on getting up the next morning played about with his fellows as if nothing had ever been the matter with his arm, not even having it in a sling.

The next day he was sent to the doctor to show him his arm, and when he entered his house, the doctor noticed, to his surprise, that the boy took hold of a chair with his lame hand and lifted it forward to sit down upon. Taking the little fellow by the hand, he then asked him if he felt any pain in his arm or hand, and the boy answered frankly that he did not. The doctor bent his fingers and saw that he had free use of them, then examined his hand and wrist and saw that there was no sign of swelling, and declared that it was the power of God which had healed the broken limb, for nothing else could have done it in so short a time.

This incident probably influenced Dr. Tate in favor of the Latter-day Saints, as he soon afterwards joined the Church. He was baptized by Elder John E. Page, and ordained an elder, and for some time was quite a faithful and efficient member, but he subsequently lost the faith. He had abundant evidence, however, while he remained in the Church that the power of God was with the Saints, as he saw it manifested on several occasions so plainly that he could not deny it. But he may have been like some others of whom it has been said that they joined the Church through seeing a miracle performed, and apostatized because they could not see one every day.

"Remarkable Healings," *Early Scenes in Church History* (Eighth book of the Faith-promoting Series, Salt Lake City: Juvenile Instructor Office, 1882), pp. 72-73.

THE LAME SHALL WALK

Elder Matthew Cowley

I was down on the Indian reservation when I met a sister who had just joined the Church, a beautiful Navajo woman. My, they dress beautifully down there. Beautiful velvet dresses. . . . They get on these beautiful dresses and go out and buy their groceries at the trading post. Anyway, after I'd met this sister, one of the missionaries called me off to the side and said, "A few months ago, my companion and I went into a hogan and that lady, that Indian sister, was lying on the ground on a sheepskin. She had been lying there for six long years. We called on her, and when we were leaving, she called us back and said in broken English, 'Isn't there something you do for sick people?'

"And we said, 'Yes.'

"She said, 'Please do it for me.' "

So they got down on their knees and administered to her, by the authority of the priesthood and in the name of Jesus Christ. Then they left, and they weren't away fifty yards, when she came out of the hogan after them and said, "Come back and see what you have done for me."

She walked. God does have control of all of these elements. You and I can reach out, and if it's his will, we can bring those elements under our control for his purposes.

> From an address delivered at the Brigham Young University, February 18, 1953.

HOLY GHOST

Now, if you have the Holy Ghost with you . . . I can say unto you that there is no greater gift, there is no greater blessing, there is no greater testimony given to any man on earth. You may have the administration of angels; you may see many miracles; you may see many wonders in the earth; but I claim that the gift of the Holy Ghost is the greatest gift that can be bestowed upon man.

—Wilford Woodruff, *Deseret Weekly News,* 38:451

LEAVE FOR WEST BERLIN TODAY
Dieter Berndt

In 1960, I was living near Hamburg in West Germany and was called to be the mission YMMIA president. Half of the members of our mission lived in East Germany, which necessitated having counterpart Young Men's and Young Ladies' presidents serving in the same capacity in East Germany. Because the Church members were scattered over a large area, we made a special effort to plan as many activities as possible that could be attended by all the youth of the mission. This presented some problems peculiar to our mission, since half the mission was in West Germany and West Berlin, and the other half was behind the iron curtain. It was impossible to hold any activities in the eastern sector, so we scheduled all of our programs in West Berlin so that the East Germans could also attend. They could easily board a subway in East Berlin, ride across the border into West Berlin and attend the meeting, then return to their homes without difficulty.

Shortly after I was called to this position, we began planning for our most important and largest activity of the year, which was to be a youth conference to be held in West Berlin during the Easter holiday. I began corresponding with the Young Men's and Young Women's presidents in East Germany and managed to complete all the arrangements for the conference by mail.

The conference was a tremendous success—very inspiring and very enjoyable. For me, the most interesting part on the program was a musical number by a very attractive and talented young lady—the Young Women's president from East Germany with whom I had been corresponding.

I immediately took advantage of the first opportunity to become acquainted with Gisaliela and was even more impressed with her as I got to know her. During the months that followed, our correspondence continued, and before long we began meeting in West Berlin whenever possible. We began to make plans for our future together and made the necessary unauthorized arrangements for her to come to Hamburg to meet my family during her vacation. Gisaliela's mother was to accompany her to East Berlin on Tuesday, August 15, where they would spend the night with her brother before continuing on to West Berlin to pick up their airline tickets for Hamburg.

The Sunday morning before Gisaliela was due to arrive, Mother and I attended church services in Hamburg as usual, but the priesthood meeting did not proceed as usual—it was announced that the Berlin Wall had been put up during the night and *all* traffic between East and West Berlin had been terminated! I was heartsick. The girl I wanted to marry was in East Germany and she would not be permitted to leave. This meant that we could not be married as we had planned.

I was so upset by this news that I decided that I would leave immediately for West Berlin to see if there was something that I could do to make arrangements for Gisaliela to leave East Germany. Knowing full well the futility of trying to deal with the Communist-controlled government, Mother told me that there was no point in my going to Berlin, for she was sure that there was nothing I could do.

I was very discouraged and dejected that Sunday morning as Mother and I knelt in prayer and asked the Lord for his help. We hoped, and prayed fervently, that somehow the Lord would help us so that Gisaliela and I could be reunited.

I was so disheartened that I couldn't concentrate on what any of the speakers had to say or on the lessons. I returned home and found that a telegram from Gisaliela was waiting for me. I couldn't believe it—she was in *West* Berlin! It was unbelievable, incomprehensible! She was not due in West Berlin for several more days!

The following Friday Gisaliela arrived at the Hamburg airport. She then told me the following story of how she came to be in West Berlin on that Saturday afternoon a few hours before the Berlin Wall went up:

"Saturday morning I was busy preparing for a district meeting when my father came into the room and said, 'I want you to leave for West Berlin today.' I replied that Mother and I had made all the arrangements to leave on Tuesday, and besides, I had to prepare for the district meeting, but my father insisted that we leave for West Berlin immediately! When I asked for a reason why we should leave early, his only reply was that he didn't know why—he just *knew* that we should leave as soon as possible.

"I couldn't understand this—it was so unlike my father to irrationally and illogically make this type of decision. I asked him again for a good reason and he said, 'I can't give you a good reason. I just have this uneasy feeling and I feel impressed that you should leave now for West Berlin.' He refused to discuss the matter further and told my mother that she was to leave with me and cautioned us not to make any stops along the way.

"He was so determined that Mother and I decided to do as he asked. We packed our bags and were on the next train to Berlin. We found out later that this was the last train we could have taken to Berlin. There were no more tickets sold after that train departed.

"We had previously planned to spend our first evening in East Berlin with my brother and in a day or two cross over into West Berlin and pick up our airline tickets at a friend's home. For some reason, we decided to continue on to the friend's house to pick up the tickets, with the intention of returning to East Berlin that evening and spending the night. However, when we picked up the tickets our friend suggested that we spend the night, so, quite contrary to our plans, we accepted the invitation and spent the night in West Berlin.

"You can imagine the shock we experienced when we awoke the next morning and found that the Berlin Wall had gone up during the night and the border had been closed. Even now, it's hard to comprehend that such a thing could actually happen. I'm so very grateful that my Heavenly Father inspired my earthly father to have me leave the day before the wall was constructed. I'm also thankful that I was obedient and listened to his inspired advice.

"Mother, of course, wanted to be with my father, who was the branch president, so she returned to East Germany that morning. We parted with heavy hearts, not knowing when, or if ever we would see each other again."

When Gisaliela related her experience to me, I knew that the Lord had opened the way for us to be married and that our marriage would be very special, and it has been.

The Lord has truly blessed us and allowed us to be brought together by forces that cannot be explained by human powers. The power of the Holy Ghost to guide and inspire each of us is real. Gisaliela and I can bear witness that this is so, for our lives have been altered dramatically by obeying the promptings of the still small voice. A miracle was truly performed in our behalf.

A MESSAGE FROM THE HEART

C. Steven Hatch

Our eldest daughter, Sharon, recently returned from her mission to France and Belgium, had decided to spend the summer in Anchorage, Alaska, with her missionary companion, Cindy Phillips. She had obtained a position as a clerk at the Travelodge in Anchorage, and was apparently having a wonderful summer, for she decided to delay her return home to Provo and her studies in the honors program at BYU until the following spring semester.

On September 17, I received a phone call from Alaska informing me that Sharon and a friend had been on a short plane trip and had failed to return. A storm had come up and the possibility of their being down somewhere safe was being held out.

I was in hopes that I would shortly receive another phone call telling me that all was well—that Sharon and her friend had been found and had not sustained any injuries, that I could spare my wife and the younger children the anxiety that I was experiencing. I confided the experience and my concern only to my son Steven, who had also filled a mission in France.

It took until the next day about 11:00 P.M. for another telephone communication. At that time, Cindy told me that search parties had been out all that day, but had not been able to identify any downed aircraft or wreckage as the weather was so bad. The search had ended for the day due to darkness, but the search would be resumed again the following morning. As it was also possible that the plane could have been safely down and Sharon would not have been able to contact Cindy to assure her of her safety because communications are so poor in the remote areas of Alaska, the possibility that Sharon was alive and well was very real.

By this time I felt that I had to inform my wife and the rest of the family of our concern for Sharon. We united in fasting and prayer and during the following day we had the opportunity to review the patriarchal blessing which Brother Sandgrin had given Sharon before she had gone to Alaska. In the blessing, she was promised that she would be sealed in the temple to a faithful companion. From this we took considerable reassurance that all *had* to be well with Sharon.

About nine o'clock that evening, we received another phone call from Anchorage, this time with Cindy's father, Brother Phillips, on the line informing us that the wreckage of the plane had been sighted and Sharon had been killed.

We were stunned, grief-stricken, tearful and yet somewhat composed at this tragic news; that is, except for our fourteen-year-old daughter Mary Ellen, who simply could not accept the reality of Sharon's death. She insisted that Sharon was too young and too good to have been taken. She began pleading with me to please contact President Harold B. Lee or one of the apostles to inquire if it really was the will of the Lord that Sharon's life be cut so short, and if not, that we ask them to command Sharon to return!

In my desire to comfort my grieving daughter, I expressed to her my feelings that in the plan of things all was well with Sharon, and that Sharon was one of those choice few that were well prepared for this step in our progression. With that assurance, Mary Ellen seemed quieter. She then went to her room and, unknown to us, wrote the following letter:

"Dear President Lee,

"I don't want to take up your valuable time, but I need to ask a favor, if you please would.

"This Thursday, my sister was found dead in an airplane out of Anchorage, Alaska. She had been missing since Tuesday. All our family had fasted and prayed for her. My father says that it is the Lord's will, and I would like to believe him, but she was so young and good. I've heard that sometimes people die when they still have work to do here.

"What I would like to ask of you is, if you would pray, or have some other General Authority pray, to see if this is the right thing, or if she could be commanded to return. Whatever you tell me I would try to believe because you are a prophet of God.

"Thank you for taking the time to read this.

"Love,
"Mary Ellen Hatch"

Mary Ellen was calmer as she rejoined the family, and we all joined hands and kneeled about our king-sized bed for family prayers that night.

The next day we began to receive telephone calls from friends who wished to express their love and sympathy to us as a family, which was very comforting. Later that evening, about nine o'clock, the telephone rang. When I answered, the voice on the other end said, "This is Harold B. Lee."

I recovered from my surprise soon enough to summon the other members of the family, who hurried to the four telephones we have at the house. With two of us at each phone, we listened as President Lee expressed his love and his recognition of how we felt. He explained that he too had very suddenly lost his own precious daughter, who had also lived in Provo. This had come as a terrible shock to him, and again he reminded us that he knew of our feelings. He went on to point out to us that the blessings which are promised to the faithful will not be curtailed because of the short span of mortality. President Lee then assured us that Sharon's promised blessings would not be curtailed and that *all* of them would be fulfilled. He reminded us that birth into this life was not the beginning nor death the end of life in the eternities, and that all the blessings to the faithful would be fulfilled. He again expressed his love for us and gave us the assurance that all was indeed well with Sharon.

As President Lee hung up the phone, Mary Ellen ran into the kitchen, threw her arms around me, and said, "Daddy that's all I needed. He answered every question I had asked him in my letter!"

We were not aware that Mary Ellen had written to the prophet. When we questioned her about it, she went to her room and returned with the letter. "I didn't mail the letter, Daddy," she said. "He must have heard the message from my heart!"

DIRECTED BY THE HOLY SPIRIT
Elder Milton R. Hunter

A few years ago late on an April afternoon, three other men and I got out of a small dugout boat at Agua Azul, Chiapas, Mexico, on the Usumacinta River. We entered a small one-motor plane to fly hundreds of miles westward to Tuxtla, Chiapas, on the Grijalva River.

In order to reach Tuxtla, which we had left that morning, President Earnest A. Strong from Springville, Utah, Gareth W. Lowe, manager of the New World Archaeological Foundation, William A. (Bill) Devenish, and I had to fly over one of the most dense jungles in the world and over ranges of mountains.

Heavy black clouds had settled over the jungle. We anticipated that we might run into trouble. For safety's sake our pilot, Bill, flew the plane very high to get above the clouds. We could not see the ground at any time through the dense clouds. The radio frequency at the Tuxtla airport did not match that on our plane, and so our pilot had to estimate our course back to Tuxtla.

We had traveled a few hours when darkness came on with the immediacy it does in the tropics. Suddenly, the Holy Spirit told me that we had crossed the Grijalva River and were headed westward from Tuxtla toward a range of mountains and that if we did not change our course quickly we would all get killed.

I immediately told Bill that we were going the wrong direction, that we had crossed the Grijalva River some distance up the river south of Tuxtla. Bill tried to determine the proper course, but because of the turbulent weather conditions, he was unable to do so.

A very depressing, dark feeling came over me. It was a feeling of gloom and despair. I said to President Strong, "We are going to be killed if we keep going in this direction. We're headed for destruction. If Bill doesn't change the direction of the plane soon, we will crash."

President Strong said that he had an oppressive feeling also. We were sitting in the back seat, and Bill heard our conversation. He asked, "President Hunter, which direction do you think we ought to go?"

I quickly replied, "Turn immediately to the right and go north."

Bill turned the plane to the right. A sweet, peaceful feeling came into my heart, and the Holy Spirit let me know that all would be well. I said, "Everything will be all right with us now. We shall arrive safely at Tuxtla without any mishap." We had not traveled very long before we saw lights shining from Tuxtla. We circled over the small, dirt airstrip with the lanterns showing us where to land. It was by now very dark.

Our plane landed safely. We observed that there were three or four hundred people at the airstrip. President Strong's son Bert, also a stake president, was there and was delighted to see us back safe. We asked Bert why so many people had collected at the airstrip that evening. He informed us that three Mexicans had gone in a two-motor plane across the jungles and mountains to the Usumacinta River that morning about the time we had flown there. They had not returned and the people of Tuxtla were out waiting for them. Some months later Gareth Lowe wrote informing us that the Mexican plane and its occupants had hit a mountain, and all were killed.

Thus, our lives were spared by heeding the directions given to us by the Holy Spirit. When we arrived at our hotel, we kneeled down and thanked God for his guidance and for saving our lives. . . .

After our return to the hotel, I became quite ill during the night. The next morning my traveling companions came to my bedroom to see why I had not come to breakfast. I told them I was too ill to get out of bed. They said that they would eat breakfast and then go down to the airstrip and look at the plane to see that everything was all right.

They soon returned and informed me that clouds had settled down on the airstrip and on Tuxtla so heavily that we would not be able to get out. We were fogged in, and they had been informed that the airstrip would probably be fogged in for a considerable time because the rainy season was beginning. They asked me what should be done.

After thinking for a few moments I was impressed by the Holy Spirit to say, "Give me a blessing and we will fly out today." At first they replied, "President Hunter, you are too ill to fly." But I insisted on being blessed. President Strong anointed and his son Bert sealed the anointing and gave me a blessing. I immediately got up out of bed, went in and ate breakfast, and felt completely healed.

We took our luggage and went down to the airstrip. Shortly after, the clouds lifted sufficiently for us to fly out. We heard later from the archaeological workman that several days passed before the fog and clouds lifted again. Therefore, that particular day was our time to fly out of Tuxtla.

On the way home President Strong said, "President Hunter, write an article for the Church magazines on this marvelous experience we have had. You were directed by the Holy Spirit as strongly as Wilford Woodruff was when he was told to get out of bed and move the wagon in the night. He followed the promptings of the Holy Spirit and moved the wagon just before a strong turbulence came along and pulled up the tree exactly where his wagon had been standing. He and his companion would have been killed if he hadn't followed the promptings of the Holy Spirit. We have had a similar experience. By following the promptings of the Holy Spirit, our lives were saved."

Youth of the Church, if you will try to keep all of God's commandments, then through the promptings of the Holy Spirit you will be guided at critical times in your lives just as we were. Your lives may also be saved by the guidance of the Holy Spirit and by the power of the Lord.

Milton R. Hunter, "Directed by the Holy Spirit," *New Era,* September 1973, pp. 4-5.

WHISPERINGS OF THE SPIRIT
Catherine A. Martin

I remember the first time I saw the little shop. As I walked past the little picture-framing shop on Fannin Street in Houston, Texas, I had the strangest feeling—something I cannot describe—that seemed to say to me that there was someone in that shop that should be a member of the Church. I was in a hurry, though, so I went on, telling myself that I would stop the next time. I passed the little shop several more times, and each time I would have this strong feeling telling me that I should go inside. It seemed that I was always in a hurry and, for one reason or another, could not stop. One day following a dental appointment, I decided to leave my car parked and walked to the office. In so doing, I passed the shop on foot and was practically pulled inside by this overwhelming sensation that there was something of spiritual interest within.

Opening the door, I heard a bell chime and as I looked around I could see picture frames of all shapes and sizes, as well as some antique frames of iron which fascinated me. As I viewed these items, a little gentleman with gray-streaked hair entered the room. While he seemed a nice fellow, I did not get a strong feeling that he was the one that I was being guided to. I continued to look for someone else, but saw no one.

As I glanced around the room once more, a painting on the wall caught my eye. It was one of a series of drawings of soldiers in different uniforms. Something told me that it was the artist who had done these drawings that I should talk with about the gospel!

I asked the shop proprietor if he could possibly give me the address of the artist. He hesitated and said that the artist had insisted that he never give out any more information than just his name, but then said, "You know, I have a feeling that this time he would not mind. I will call him and give him your name and phone number."

The artist, James C. Whittington, did call me and we decided to meet and discuss art and history. Of course, I also had in mind a far more eternal subject to discuss with Mr. Whittington. I found Mr. Whittington to be a nice-looking gentleman with a very pleasant smile. While he was friendly, I could also sense that here was a man of firm conviction, not easily swayed, who would evaluate and study thoroughly before reaching decisions in any important areas of his life.

I remember saying to him that I knew something that he should know—something that would change his entire life for the better. He was interested in just what that could be. So, with such encouragement, I proceeded to tell him about the restoration of Christ's Church upon the earth. I told him about my search for the truth and the desire I had to know what the Lord would have me be. Then I told him about the strange and wonderful events that led to my discovery of the gospel and the beauty that entered my life at the same time.

What I perceived in Mr. Whittington was true; he was receptive to what had been said, but he reserved the right to study and evaluate before giving any response. Mr. Whittington was open, honest, and diligent in his efforts to know the truth, and in the face of much outside opposition was baptized by Elders LaRoy Thompson and Glen Higley on July 18, 1969. The wonderful part about this story is that James is still active and faithful in the gospel, fulfilling his callings with love and growing more every day toward his spiritual goals.

The Lord truly knows and loves each one of us. He knows those that are ready to hear his word and if we are prayerful and will perform our duty he will guide us to those righteous individuals. I have had some beautiful experiences through the whisperings of the Spirit, which is a gift available to all of us if only we will love and value another's exaltation as our own.

PROMPTINGS OF THE STILL SMALL VOICE

Benjamin F. Johnson

[On June 22, 1882, the Benjamin Franklin Johnson company started on their long journey south to Arizona. Because they were late in starting, the Johnson company had to go one hundred miles out of their way in order to find a safe place to cross the Rio Virgin River, which was swollen from the spring run-off. The weather was extremely hot, and the deep sands and winding river slowed their travel and made the journey perilous.

One evening about a week after their departure, as they were looking for a suitable camping spot, the company came upon a beautiful open space near the river, with apparently every facility for camping. The group was eager to stop here, but Benjamin felt prompted otherwise. Benjamin tells us:]

"I drove my light vehicle over the green grass that was so inviting, and stopped to look around, but a voice within me said, 'Go on.'

"I looked ahead and saw a high ridge to go over, and my feelings said, 'No,' but the voice said, 'Go on over the ridge.'

"My hand involuntarily drew the mules back to the road, even while I was wondering why I did so, for I feared all the other members of the company would be greatly disturbed at my decision not to stop at the only inviting spot we had seen in many days. But I went on, with the company following my lead up and down a long, rocky, dry way. After going nearly two miles we came upon a high table of flat rock, which offered nothing inviting, but safety.

"Here we camped, and I greatly feared I had offended everyone in the company, but much to my relief nothing was said, and we put our stock up on higher ground. We soon heard thunder with fearful lightning and wind—a tempest was upon us which continued till near daylight with a dreadful roaring. In the morning, we saw that the valley was flooded with rolling waves of mud, from mountain to mountain. We beheld the fearful picture with wondering astonishment, and with joy and gratitude to God and the promptings of the still small voice that led us to the only safe spot in that valley for many miles. Had we camped at the place first chosen, everything we possessed would have been overwhelmed and destroyed.

"We later learned that a wagon loaded with salt had camped there that night, and the teamster narrowly escaped with his life, losing his wagon and load."

Benjamin Franklin Johnson, *My Life's Review,* p. 275.

"TAKE YOUR MONEY OUT OF YOUR PURSE!"

One day, in 1903, the Northern States Mission president's wife, Mary Smith Ellsworth, was taking a deposit of three hundred dollars to the bank, which belonged to the mission and the missionaries. As she passed through a crowded department store in downtown Chicago, she heard a warning voice: "Take your money out of your purse!"

She turned to the young English girl who was with her at the time and asked if she had said anything.

"No, Mum," was the reply.

When the voice came a second time, she repeated the message to the girl, who said: "I'd certainly do what it said, Mum."

So she stepped behind a large screen, took the money out of her wallet, wrapped it inside a handkerchief, and pinned it inside of her dress front.

As they finished their shopping and were walking out of the store, Mary felt a tug on her purse. She looked down and saw that it was open—and her wallet was gone. Looking around, she saw a small boy scurrying away through the crowd, carrying her wallet.

It was later learned that the little boy was a member of a group of clever young boys who were being trained and directed by expert pickpockets. Had Mary not followed the advice of her young English companion to do what the voice said, the young pickpocket would have made off with the missionaries' money that they desperately needed for their living expenses that month.

From the biography of Mary Rachel Smith Ellsworth (unpublished manuscript in the possession of Jaynann M. Payne, Provo, Utah), pp. 10-11.

MISSIONARIES

There can be no greater or more important calling for man than that in which the elders of The Church of Jesus Christ of Latter-day Saints are engaged when in the discharge of their duties as missionaries to the world.

—Joseph F. Smith, *Millennial Star,* 37:408, June 28, 1875

YOU ARE TO LEAVE ZUNI BY TOMORROW
Wayne Meyers

In the spring of 1949, I was teaching the missionary class in Sugar City, Idaho. I wanted to encourage these young men to accept the responsibilities and blessings of a mission, so I promised them that if twenty of the class members would accept mission calls before the summer was over, their teacher would follow their excellent example and also go on a mission. They enthusiastically accepted my challenge and by fall twenty-three young men from our ward had responded affirmatively to mission calls.

True to my promise, I conveyed to the bishop my desire and willingness to go on a mission. Shortly thereafter, I received my mission call and notification of an interview with Elder Matthew Cowley. Elder Cowley told me that he had desired to send me to New Zealand where he and I had served before, but they were opening up a mission among the Lamanite people so he was going to send me to the Navajo-Zuni Mission. His only counsel to me was to teach these Lamanite brothers and sisters the gospel so that I could use the power of the priesthood to lay hands on them and bless them. With that instruction, I packed my sleeping bag, kissed my dear wife and two-year-old son goodbye, and left for mission headquarters in Gallup, New Mexico.

A few months later I was assigned a new companion and a new field of labor—Zuni, Arizona. Missionaries had been sent to Zuni before, but had left without having converted any of the Zuni tribe to the gospel. I was determined that with the Lord's help I would baptize many of my Lamanite brothers and bring them into the kingdom to receive the blessings of the priesthood, just as Elder Cowley had instructed me to do.

The Zuni Indians are very talented craftsmen—and very religious. They work their farms during the warm summer months, then move back into town for the winter where they concentrate on working on their crafts and participating in religious ceremonies and rites. At the age of eight, the children participate in a ceremonial-type baptism in which the child is first cleansed and purified by driving all the evil influences out of his body. This is accomplished by literally beating the "devil" out of the child. A whip made from the reeds that grow in the nearby river is administered in rather strong terms by the witch doctor until the evil spirits become so uncomfortable that they gladly depart the body, thus leaving the child purified and worthy to join in the religious order of the tribe.

My heart went out to the child participating in this ceremony, but I was also quite impressed by the fact that the Zunis had retained a form of the true teachings of their forefathers and were performing a "baptism" for all of their eight-year-old children.

I felt that if I was to reach these people with my message of the restored gospel and its true ordinances I had to know more about the Zuni beliefs and religious practices. So, for several nights, as the Zunis gathered in the town square and began their religious ceremonies, I positioned myself on the roof of one of the nearby homes so that I could have an unobstructed view of all that transpired. I knew that the Zunis regarded these ceremonies as sacred, but what I did not know was that the ceremonies were also secret!

Several days later I received word that the Zuni Council had met and that it was their pleasure that I attend the next Council meeting. This was joyful news! I was sure that the Lord had touched their hearts and therefore they had invited me to the Council so that I could truly begin my work among the Zuni people by teaching the gospel to the leaders of their nation.

I was one very happy missionary as I entered the Council room, eager and ready to begin the work of my ministry. I was greeted and ushered into an area where eight or ten men sat in a circle discussing some matter in the Zuni language. My presence was ignored as the conversation progressed into a heated argument. Finally, when my curiosity could no longer be contained, I asked the man seated nearest me what the conversation was about.

"Well, Elder Meyers," he said, "they want you to leave the village. You and the doctrines that you preach are no longer welcome among our people. It has been decided that you are to leave Zuni by tomorrow night."

Nothing further was said by any of the Indians in the circle. They simply nodded their approval of what had been said and silently left the Council room.

I was heartsick. It appeared that my missionary labors among the Zuni people were going to end before I had even begun to preach the gospel. I confided my problems to Grant Hamblin, the owner of the trading post, who was also LDS. When I described the member of the Zuni Council who had told me that I was to leave the village, he stated, "That's Willy Zuni, the worst trouble-maker we have in town! I'd stay away from him! You'd better solve your problems some other way than to try to reason with Willy Zuni!"

Nighttime, the time the Council had set for my premature departure from Zuni was fast approaching and I was at a loss to know what to do, so I called the mission president in Gallup, New Mexico.

"You are not to leave Zuni!" President Flake stated emphatically. "We've worked for many years to get missionaries in there and now that we're there, we're going to stay! Don't give in to their demands and I'll be there tomorrow and see what I can do."

We knew that President Flake would do all that he possibly could to help us once he arrived, but we also knew that we needed the help of the Lord if we were to remain in Zuni. So that night, as my companion and I knelt beside our beds, we prayed to the Lord and asked him to show us what he would have us do so that we could stay among the Zuni people and carry out our missionary work. We then retired for the night, comforted by the assurance that the Lord would answer our prayer and somehow the way would be opened to us.

I had not been asleep very long when I had one of the most glorious experiences of my life. A vision opened before my eyes and I was shown what I must do to stay in Zuni and continue my missionary labors. In the vision I saw a man, obviously a Lamanite, sitting on a rough-hewn bench holding a little girl in his arms. I then recognized him as the man I sat beside in the Council meeting, the one who had told me that I was to leave Zuni! I received the very strong impression that I should go to his home and talk to him; then, without further explanation, the vision closed and I returned to sleep.

When I awoke the next morning, I was almost beside myself with happiness. I had never before been blessed with a revelation from the Lord and I was positively elated at having our prayers answered in such a miraculous manner. With grateful hearts my companion and I again knelt beside our bed to thank our Heavenly Father for this choice blessing and the knowledge of what we must do to continue with our missionary work.

I had just begun to pray when my voice was taken from me and I could no longer utter a word! A very stifling and confining feeling came over me and I felt as though each breath would be my last. I have never experienced anything so terrifying in all my life. After having this limited experience with the powers of darkness, I can now appreciate how the Prophet Joseph must have felt just prior to the time he received the visitation from the Father and the Son, when the adversary unleashed his *full* powers upon him. I felt that I would surely succumb at any moment, and began praying with all my heart that I would be relieved of this terrifying condition. Much to my relief this power of darkness then left me— at least the power that bound my mouth departed—but I was left with a very desperate and depressed feeling. In fact, I was so depressed that had it not been for the sustaining encouragement of my companion I would have gladly forsaken my sacred calling as a missionary and taken up my sleeping bag and walked back to Sugar City and my wife and child. The joy and happiness I had experienced only a few moments before was gone and I felt as though I had been given over to the buffetings and temptations of the adversary.

I didn't give in to those feelings of despair and depression, and my companion and I set out to find out where Willy Zuni lived. We inquired at the trading post and were questioned by Grant Hamblin as to our reason for wanting to know of Willy Zuni's whereabouts. I told him that I wished to discuss the Council's decision with Willy Zuni.

"Well, I think you had better forget about discussing it with Willy Zuni," he replied. "I definitely would not go to his house. In fact, I would leave him completely alone."

"But," I protested, "I've been told by the Lord that I should go and talk to Willy Zuni."

"Well, maybe you had better go then," he agreed.

My companion and I followed his directions to Willy's home where, with rather uncertain feelings, we knocked on the door. When a voice invited us in, we entered and found Willy Zuni seated on a bench holding his little daughter on his lap—just as I had seen in the dream the night before.

"Come in and sit down, Elder Meyers," he said. "I've been expecting you. I knew that you would be coming to see me today."

I was not quite prepared for this, but before I could question him as to how he knew I was coming to see him, he asked, "Do you know who I am?"

"I know that your name is Willy Zuni," I replied, "but other than that I know nothing about you."

"I am the spiritual leader of the Zuni tribe. Elder Meyers, the people do not want you here any more and they have decided that you must leave town, but I have been impressed that you should stay. I will see that you are not driven out of our village. You will stay in Zuni!"

This was one command from the Council that I was glad to obey.

From that time on, my companion and I were welcomed into the homes of the Zuni people. We had the choice blessing of teaching many of these Lamanite brothers and sisters the gospel and were then able to use our priesthood to bless them—just as Elder Cowley had instructed me to do.

With the Lord's help, we were able to accomplish a great work and overcome many obstacles—including the adversary.

THE "VOICE" OF THE LORD

Robert Nixon

Elder Marvin and I had been doing some part-member family work in Carlton, one of the better sections of Nottingham, England, when we became acquainted with Sister Williams.

When the missionaries had first knocked on their door four years earlier, both Mr. and Mrs. Williams invited the elders into their home and began the discussions. They were exceptionally receptive to the gospel, especially Mr. Williams, until the missionaries presented the third discussion, which involves the Word of Wisdom. Mr. Williams enjoyed both smoking and drinking. The missionaries' suggestion that he should give these up was just too much—he gave up the gospel instead! He invited the elders to leave his home and forbade them to ever come back.

Mr. Williams turned completely negative towards the Church and would refuse discussion anytime the Church was mentioned. By this time his wife had a testimony of the gospel and wanted to continue with the lessons, but he would not allow her to have the elders in the home. Having gained a very strong testimony of the Church, Mrs. Williams requested her husband's permission to be baptized. He refused and the first of many arguments over the subject began.

After one of their arguments, he began to seriously reflect on what was happening to his family. "I am losing my wife to this Church," he thought. "It has come between us and divided us. I guess I'm going to have to accept her baptism and try to make the most of it, if I want to keep my wife."

He decided that he would allow her to be baptized. As he did, a very strange thing happened. All of a sudden a very calm, sweet, peaceful feeling came over him. "It's just a release of tension," he thought, but Mrs. Williams had exactly the same experience happen to her at the same time while she was lying in bed upstairs.

Sister Williams was baptized and had been a member of the Church for about a year and a half when I met her. Mr. Williams had allowed her to attend all of the meetings except sacrament meeting, which was held across town. He had even permitted the missionaries to come to their home and discuss the gospel with her—after he had left the room.

One day Sister Williams said to me, "I'd like you to come to my home and talk to my husband. He seems to be softening in his attitude towards the Church."

We made it a point to stop by the Williamses' home whenever we were in the neighborhood, hoping that we would find him home. He was very courteous and friendly the first time we met him, and we were very impressed with him. He was quite a dynamic and capable young man and we knew he would be a great asset to the Church in that area. His first greeting to us was, "I want you to know that you're *never* going to get me into the Church!" This was said in a joking manner, but we knew he was serious.

We continued to stop by and discuss his favorite pastime, which was soccer. He had begun playing on one of the local teams, so he decided to swim three nights a week and give up drinking beer so that he could get back in shape. As time went on, we could feel that he was at least accepting us as friends, although all of our discussions were on sports and other items of interest to him— never on the Church. One evening I surprised myself *and* Mr. Williams by interrupting the subject we were discussing, and saying, "Brother Williams, why aren't you a member of the Church?"

This really caught him off guard. He sat back in his chair, was silent and thoughtful for a minute, and then he said, "Because I cannot give up smoking."

"Brother Williams," I said, "is that all that is holding you back?"

"Yes," he replied. "I'd love to be a member of the Church. I want to get my family back together. I just can't give up smoking so I can be baptized."

Sister Williams, who was in the kitchen at the time preparing refreshments, overheard and nearly dropped the dishes she was holding!

"Brother Williams," I said, "I know that with the Lord's help you can give up smoking." His eyes began to sparkle and his countenance brightened as the Spirit filled the room. I knew then that he would be baptized.

We told him that we would be back to visit him the next week and would start teaching him the lessons to prepare him for baptism. He agreed, so we gave him the first two discussions which were on the Book of Mormon and the apostasy and restoration. The third lesson was a discussion on the Word of Wisdom. We knew this would be a difficult and critical point in the progression of Brother Williams.

During the week between the second and third discussion, I caught a severe cold which rapidly progressed into bronchitis and a strep throat. My throat was raw and very painful. I couldn't speak—in fact, all I could manage was a hoarse whisper, which was extremely painful at that. I knew that somehow I had to teach this important lesson on the Word of Wisdom because my companion was new in the field and didn't know the discussion yet. I was very worried and concerned as to how I was going to manage this meeting, so I asked the Lord for his help. As we drove up in front of the Williamses' home, we stopped for a few moments and I silently offered another prayer. I then tried to give my companion some instructions, but I couldn't talk.

My companion greeted them at the door and we were invited to come in and sit down. I opened my flannel board to begin the discussion and as I did, the pain in my throat left me! I began speaking easily and clearly in a rich, full, strong voice. I have never delivered a more powerful or effective discussion, or one in which the Spirit of the Lord seemed to be guiding and inspiring every word that was spoken. After I completed the presentation, we challenged Brother Williams to live the Word of Wisdom and set a date for his baptism, which he accepted. He then closed the meeting with prayer—the most humble and touching prayer I've ever heard.

I folded up my flannel board and my throat immediately became raw again, only more intense than before. I couldn't even speak to say goodnight to the Williamses as we left.

"Either you were going through extreme agony while giving the discussion," my companion said, "or else the Lord certainly was with you."

I wasn't in agony. I felt nothing but the comforting Spirit of the Lord as I gave that lesson.

Brother Williams was baptized sixteen days later, on Thanksgiving Day. Within nine months he was made an elder, and shortly thereafter he was set apart as the branch president. He was just what the Lord needed to build up the Church in that area. Brother

Williams was tremendous in the way he magnified his calling, just as the Lord knew he would be. The Lord had plans for David Williams in his kingdom and that is why I believe I was blessed with the ability to give that all-important discussion when I couldn't speak on my own.

The Lord often speaks through his servants, and this time he did so literally.

THE PLANE WILL GET DOWN SAFELY!

On November 3, 1973, a great winged shadow bumped swiftly across the tortured grey landscape of the Gila wilderness in New Mexico. Six miles above, the interrupted sunlight shone on the back of a National Airlines DC10 jetliner that seemed to hang in the four o'clock blue afternoon while the world moved underneath. Inside, just in front of the craft's eastern wing, Elder Leonard Dobson was riding home in style.

While the ragged mountains slipped away under his right elbow, he relaxed, reading a little from the book of 2 Nephi in his battered Spanish-language Book of Mormon and turning occasionally to snap a photo from his cabin window.

And sometimes he just leaned back and thought about some of the wonderful people he was leaving behind in the Venezuela Mission where he had served faithfully for two years, and he thought, perhaps, of an LDS lawyer in Sonora, California, who had given a copy of the Book of Mormon to a twenty-six-year-old non-Mormon civil engineer named Leonard Dobson.

A brief year as a member, a mission call, the mission (could it really have been two years?), and now he was sitting on a six-mile-high cushion of air, waiting for the red and yellow lights of the San Francisco airport to come and gather him home.

Suddenly the sleepy rumble of the three jet engines was shattered by a deafening explosion; far below the huge shadow faltered; inside the plane there were screams of shock and horror, quickly dying into stunned silence.

"I looked back over my left shoulder into the cabin area to see what had happened, because it sounded like the explosion was in back of me," Leonard reports. "Then I looked back over my right shoulder and saw the engine coming apart, pieces falling away, and flames. My first thought was, 'Oh no; you're going to be one of those people who go in a big airplane crash.' The very first thing I did was pray. It just didn't make any sense for me to die at that time, but if I was going to I wanted to talk to my Maker about it, so I started praying."

As he prayed, all fear left him. The words, "You are a servant of the Lord Jesus Christ; the plane will get down safely," kept running through his mind. Certain passages from his patriarchal blessing also came into consciousness, reassuring him that his mission on earth was not yet completed. It was a calm and confident young man who finished his prayer and turned to see what he could do to help.

"Some passengers were screaming and some were rushing around the cabin. The stewardesses were very busy. At that time I noticed the condensation in the cabin area, a fog that looked like smoke, and I realized that I couldn't hear." He found out later that the fog and the temporary deafness both resulted from a broken window two seats back through which the cabin had decompressed.

As oxygen rushed from the cabin through the broken window, oxygen masks began dropping from their compartments overhead. Leonard's didn't drop, and he had to pry off the panel with his fingernails and remove the mask manually. Many of the masks didn't work properly.

"People were moving from one seat to another trying to find a mask that worked. Some of them were fainting, and as they fainted their arms would fall away from their faces and their masks would fall off."

There was a real spirit of brotherhood in the little airplane community, passengers helping passengers as best they could. The stewardesses moved about with amazing energy and efficiency, administering oxygen and first aid to those in need.

And so, with an engine gone, the cabin depressurized, and an ocean of thin air under them, the huge craft dipped its nose and went looking for its shadow.

"The pilot put the plane into a steep dive to get some thicker air into the cabin. I got up to help some people across the aisle who had fainted but a stewardess came to them with a portable oxygen supply and motioned for me to sit down and buckle up. They had to communicate by gestures because no one could hear."

The jet leveled off a few thousand feet above the rugged desert floor, and the passengers were told to get into crash landing position with their heads between their knees. The last thing Leonard saw before putting his head down was jagged peaks flashing by. A few minutes later they all felt the beautiful jolt of rubber against concrete. The wounded plane with one engine destroyed had managed to limp into Albuquerque, New Mexico, thanks to the skill of the crew and the blessings of the Lord.

On the ground the passengers slid to safety down emergency chutes and then embraced one another as old friends, shouting words that no one could hear.

The happiness of the occasion was marred by a tragedy that some of the passengers didn't even know about yet. The man sitting by the broken window had been sucked out of the plane by the force of the decompression. There had also been several heart attacks and cases of shock.

It was a day of stark tragedy, lightened only by the fact that according to all the laws of probability, the tragedy should have been much, much worse.

In retrospect Leonard says, "Life is a gift and is very precious. We are in the Lord's hands at all times, and we must use the life, light, and guidance we have in his service. All we have and are we owe to him."

And just as a great jet found its own shadow in the safety of the Albuquerque airport, Elder Leonard Dobson found a faint shadow of God's great love for his servants in those few terse words: "You are a servant of the Lord Jesus Christ; the plane will get down safely."

"The Plane Will Get Down Safely!",
New Era, January 1974, pp. 18-19.

A GREATER WORK IN THE SPIRIT WORLD
Thomas G. Romney

Three days out from New York the vessel on which Keith Burt was a passenger headed for the missionary field went down, and with it the young elder. His parents were irreconcilable, not being able to understand why one so full of promise and in the line of duty should thus be snatched from them. Never before had they heard of a vessel being sunk with a Mormon elder aboard.

Brother Burt, his father, was an ordinance worker in the Cardston Temple, and one day as he was in that sacred edifice, the voice of his son reached his ear admonishing him to cease mourning the departure, and assuring him that it was possible for Keith to engage in a greater work than he could do in mortality. Since Brother Burt could not see his son, he wished for an assurance that would leave no doubt in his mind that it was Keith who was addressing him. "How shall I know that you are my son speaking?"

Then came the voice declaring that on that very day Brother Burt would be called upon by President Wood, the temple president, to bear his testimony. This would be a certain and indisputable witness to the father that it was the son who had visited him.

President Wood had been engaged in the sealing room uniting families for eternity when he was "moved upon" to ask for Brother Burt to come and bear his testimony to the group. Upon inquiry, he learned that Brother Burt was in a room below changing his clothes preparatory to going home for the night. Imagine the joy that filled the heart of the father when he received the message from President Wood. No longer was there any doubt in his mind regarding the reality of the visit of his son; and with that doubt dispelled, he ceased mourning his loss.

The Gospel in Action (Salt Lake City: Deseret News Press, 1949), p. 262.

OBEDIENCE

Whatever God requires is right, no matter what it is, although we may not see the reason thereof until all of the events transpire.

—Joseph Smith, Jr.

CALLED BY THE LORD
Hazel Clark

After a long, full professional life of teaching in the public schools, and later instructing at BYU, I retired at the age of sixty-five. I had expected to continue in full activity, but I was suddenly beset with a multitude of health problems. I had always been a healthy person, and so I became rather discouraged when the doctors' treatments failed to bring me relief and comfort so that I could lead a normal life. I became even more disheartened when my doctor advised me to make the necessary preparations to enter the hospital for further testing and therapy.

I had begun packing my bag and making the necessary preparations for my stay in the hospital when the telephone rang. It was my bishop, who asked, "Hazel, would you come and see me today?" and I replied, "Oh, Bishop, I'm going to the hospital today."

"Well," he said, "on the way, come by and see me."

I was not only curious as to why he wanted to see me, but why he didn't even inquire as to why I was going to the hospital. I guess I was not the only one that had taken my health for granted for so many years.

I put my little bag in the car and my husband drove me to the church to meet with the bishop. "We'd like to call you to work in the Primary," he stated.

I was stunned. I had never worked in the Primary before, and the prospect of teaching a class of little children at the age of sixty-five was completely overwhelming, but I had never refused a church position and I was not going to now, so I told the bishop that I would be happy to accept the calling *if* I could manage the necessary strength.

During the next ten days in the hospital I had ample time to lie in bed and reflect on this new calling, and the more I thought about it, the more concerned and distressed I became. It had been just too many years since I had taught little Sunday School children and I most certainly did not feel confident about assuming a teaching position in the Primary. Due to exceedingly large numbers of young children in our ward, the bishopric had always had difficulty in staffing the organizations with teachers, so I was beginning to wonder if the bishop had called me to be a Primary teacher more out of desperation than from inspiration. "Surely," I thought, "there must be enough young people in the ward to fill these positions without calling someone my age to teach Primary."

After I had been in the hospital for several days, my bishop, who was an M.D., stopped by my room to see me while making his hospital rounds. "Well," he said, "you're going to teach Primary for us, aren't you?"

"Oh, Bishop," I thought, "can't you see that I'm too old and sick to teach Primary?" Aloud I simply replied, "I guess I will, as soon as I get well."

The bishop seemed pleased with my response and after a few pleasantries he left, seemingly totally unconcerned with the obvious possibility that I would not be able to physically undertake such a demanding calling for a person of my age.

The treatment and therapy my doctor prescribed were sufficiently effective so that within a few days I was well enough to return home, and before long I was able to attend my church meetings.

During the first sacrament meeting that I attended following my illness it was announced that those ward members who were to be set apart for their new positions were to meet in the Relief

Society room at the close of the meeting. And so, with tremendous feelings of inadequacy and anxiety, and actually not feeling too well physically, I went into the Relief Society room to be set apart as a Primary teacher. The men were busy rearranging chairs and making the necessary arrangements, so I sat patiently and waited for my turn to be set apart. As I waited, my thoughts were greatly concerned as to just how I was going to physically fulfill this calling. My mother had passed away by the time she was my age with similar health problems, and I was not all that confident that my health would be restored sufficiently that I would be strong enough to teach active youngsters.

I was deeply engrossed in my thoughts and anxieties when I felt a firm but gentle hand on my shoulder, and then my father, who had passed away ten years earlier and was very dear to me, said, "Hazel, you're going to be all right." He patted my shoulder very reassuringly, as if to emphasize that he knew all would be well with me. I was so startled that I did not turn around to see him, but I *know* he was there—his voice and touch were so special and distinctive that I could never mistake him for someone else. He is the only person I have ever known that I would really trust, and so his promise to me that I would be all right was of incalculable comfort and assurance to me. I was so touched when my father said those words that I began to weep uncontrollably and could hardly manage to walk to the chair where I was to be set apart. No one else in the room was aware of the tremendous experience I had just had, so they were a bit bewildered by my lack of composure. I knew then for a surety that I had been called by the Lord to this position and that I would be given the necessary health and strength to fulfill this calling.

I have served for three years now as a Primary teacher and have been delighted and gratified to find that I still have talents to share and a contribution to make to the ward and the building up of God's kingdom. One of my greatest joys has been to realize that, even though I am nearing seventy years of age, I still have a mission to perform here on earth.

I am so very grateful to have had this choice experience and I know that there will be other opportunities for me to serve and I will be blessed with the health to magnify these callings if I will but obediently do all that the Lord asks of me.

COUNSELLING THE LORD

Edna Ogden

During the Korean War the young men of the Church were not permitted by the government to serve on missions because they were subject to the draft. The missionary effort of the Church therefore had to fall upon the older men and some of the women of the Church. My husband, Dale, was called on a six-month mission to the Lamanite people and served in the Gallup, New Mexico, area. Shortly after he arrived home in Richfield, Utah, he was called to be the president of the Lamanite Mission in that area and I was called to serve as a stake missionary.

This was a difficult assignment. First of all, the reservations are for Indians only and they seemed to resent any white man's intrusion into their lands and their way of life. The missionaries were no exception. They were not welcomed into the Indians' dwellings or on the reservation. In fact, we frequently heard comments about the possibility of the missionaries being expelled from the reservation.

The year before we were called on our missions, the Indians began leaving the reservation to come into the Richfield area to help with the harvesting of the crops. They would live in barracks or some other quickly constructed building on the farm in which they were working. After the crops were harvested they would move on to another farm and another "new" home. The change of climate combined with poor living conditions and their lack of knowledge concerning proper sanitation procedures resulted in the death of a large number of babies and small children that first year. It was a sad situation but I didn't know what I alone could do about this overwhelming problem.

We loved the Lamanite people and did everything we could possibly think of to bring them our message of the restored gospel, but it wasn't easy. The Indians are very superstitious and reluctant to accept things that are new or different. In addition, they did not trust any white man, perhaps for good reason. It was really quite a struggle to become acquainted with them and gain their confidence enough so that they would just say hello.

Dale and I were not discouraged, though, just because the work was difficult. We were confident that if we were prayerful and diligent in our callings, the Lord would open the way before us.

One afternoon Dale had some matter he wanted to discuss with some of the Indians staying at a place we called the Carrot Farm, so I went along to keep him company. The Carrot Farm, a large farm north of Richfield, was owned by Mr. DiFiore, who raised large quantities of carrots and potatoes with the assistance of migrant labor. Dale was involved in his discussions with the Indians so I walked around and looked at the barracks and the other facilities for the migrant Indian laborers. It was sad. "No wonder the Indians lose so many of their babies when they live in this type of environment," I thought to myself.

I was deeply engrossed in my thoughts when I suddenly experienced a feeling that I have never had before nor since. I was bewildered by this strange feeling and was beginning to wonder at its cause when a voice said to me, "You can have a nursery school here and take care of the Indian babies while their mothers work. You can get food from the Welfare Program to feed these babies. You will then have contact with their mothers and much good missionary work will come from this."

"Why, that's absolutely impossible!" I thought. "I could never get those Indian mothers to leave their babies with me. They don't know me and they would never trust me to take care of their babies. And besides, the man that owns this farm would never permit it. He has some very bitter feelings about the Church and he definitely wouldn't allow Mormon missionaries to conduct any kind of a program on his property—including a nursery for babies. And this area of the farm is overcrowded now and he'd never let me have the space for a nursery. It just can't be done!"

So I talked myself out of following the counsel of the still small voice and did nothing about starting a nursery.

Dale and I continued to work with the Lamanite people that year, but with only limited success. After the crops were harvested, the Indians left Richfield and returned to their winter homes in warmer climates.

The following season the Indians returned to help with the harvest. I again accompanied Dale to the Carrot Farm and the same experience was repeated, almost word for word. It was almost as though a tape recorder was playing the message over again in my mind. And again, my reaction was the same. "It's just impossible," I thought. "It can't be done!" I shrugged and quickly dismissed the suggestion for a nursery as a total impossibility.

We returned home, and within a few days I experienced a very painful kidney stone attack. I had had these attacks before and usually after a week, or ten days at the most, I was able to pass the stone. But this time it lodged in a tube. One of my kidneys had been removed, so the blockage of my remaining kidney was serious. Death from uremic poisoning can occur in as little as twelve hours if at least one of the kidneys is not functioning.

The doctors in Richfield were unable to give me the specialized care I desperately needed, so my husband chartered a plane and flew me to Los Angeles. I received excellent care from some of the best urologists in the country, but my condition continued to deteriorate.

I suddenly became aware of new surroundings. I could plainly see that my body was still in that hospital bed, but my spirit was in a place where everything was shadowy. There were people there, but it was so misty that I couldn't see their faces. In the distance I could see a brighter land and I began walking toward it. I seemed to be free to go wherever I wished, although somehow I understood that these people could not. As I continued to walk I saw a large door and the word *baptized* was communicated to me. Yes, I had been baptized so the keeper of the gate permitted me to enter. I walked on and came to another door and this time the words *temple marriage* came to mind. I was given permission to enter, so I continued on until I came to another keeper of the gate standing beside the veil. "You may pass," he said as he tried to usher me through. "No!" I objected. "I'm not ready yet!"

"Well, why aren't you ready?" he asked.

"Because I have all these things I have to do," I replied. "I have three children and an Indian boy that I have taken to raise."

"That's not a good reason," he said. "Others can raise your children. You can't go back for that."

"But I'm not ready," I protested. "I'm just not worthy to enter here."

With that his expression became very solemn and he said, "Excuse me for a minute, please."

He began talking to someone on the other side of the veil and then a voice addressed me, saying, "You were inspired to start a nursery for those Indian children, but you didn't. Why didn't you do as you were prompted to do?"

"Oh, I will, if you will give me a little more time. I *promise* I'll do it, if you'll just let me go back," I pleaded.

Permission was granted. I returned to my body and suffered intensely. The pain continued to be almost unbearable until I was relieved of the kidney stone and then I slowly began to regain my strength. After a month's stay in the hospital I was permitted to return home to Richfield.

I was barely able to walk around on my own when I called my missionary companion and told her that we had to go out to the Carrot Farm. We met with Mr. DiFiore and told him of our desires to establish a nursery for the Indian children. We quickly pointed out how much more work the Indian women would be able to do if they did not have to tend their babies in the fields. We also mentioned that we would be bringing large amounts of good food for the Indians so that they would be healthier and if he would just let us have the nursery, he wouldn't have nearly as many problems with illness as he had had previously.

He enthusiastically agreed that a nursery would be an excellent idea. "And," he said, "if there's anything that you need for the nursery you can have it."

I was delighted, and a little surprised, but I shouldn't have been. The Lord had told me to do it and he never asks us to do anything but what he opens the way for it to be accomplished.

Mr. DiFiore provided us with the best barracks on the farm, installed a fence to make a play yard, brought in clean sand so that the children could have a sandpile to play in, and even paid one English-speaking Indian woman to translate for the Indians.

I went to the stake president and he said that I could have all the food I needed from the welfare farm. He also volunteered to deliver fresh milk every day and told me that I could have anything else that I needed. When I asked for a washing machine, he gave us *two* old ones. In the meantime, the farm owner had had water piped to the barracks and had even installed some stoves for cooking and heating. The people of Richfield were very generous in donating clothing—and their time. The Relief Society sisters helped by collecting clothing and toys for use in the nursery.

We came by the equipment we needed rather easily, but it took a good number of meetings and explanations of our plans for the nursery before we were finally under way. Before long, though, we had about thirty-five babies that the Indian women entrusted to our care.

We arrived early one morning, between 5:30 and 6:00 A.M., to find a large group of Indians waiting for us. They had arrived at the nursery camp during the night, desperately in need of help. It seems that their clothing had somehow been lost and they had resorted to wrapping their baby in an old inner-tube. We immediately built a fire, heated bath water, and had a delightful time bathing that unfortunate child and dressing it in clean, warm clothing. I couldn't help but be aware of their intense interest in *how* I did all this. It was quite obvious that I was teaching a very informal yet effective class in baby care. I was also very much aware of the sparkle in their eyes—and the tears in the eyes of the mother. My eyes were also full of tears and my heart full of gratitude for this opportunity to make my life a worthy one— a useful life. As much as this experience meant to me personally, it was even more meaningful to the advancement of our work among the Indians. From that day on the Indians were our friends. They even returned in the evenings for parties, dances, and meetings with the elders.

My mother and mother-in-law continued to care for my children while my missionary companion and I operated the nursery. The Indian babies were healthy and happy, and their mothers were most appreciative. Everything was going beautifully, then one of the Indian babies died. I was heartsick! I couldn't understand it. Hadn't I done everything that I was supposed to do to keep my part of the agreement with my Heavenly Father? What had I done wrong?

Fortunately the baby did not die while it was in our care, so the Indian mothers continued to bring their babies to the nursery, but I was still very depressed over this for several days.

One day, Mr. DiFiore and a group of five or six other men came into the fields and began a tour of the barracks area. I did not recognize any of the men other than Mr. DiFiore; however, I later learned that Mr. Bennett, who was in charge of the Bureau of Indian Affairs in Washington, D.C., and the chief of the tribe from Windowrock, Arizona, were among the group. They were trying to select a site for the new school to be constructed for the Indians.

As Mr. DiFiore explained our nursery program to the men, he was obviously very proud of our accomplishments. I was unaware of the identity of our important visitors so I went on tending the babies while I enjoyed listening to Mr. DiFiore's kind compliments.

The men left the nursery and proceeded on their tour. A few minutes later one of the Indians in the group came back to the nursery and asked me, "Are you a Mormon?"

"Yes," I replied.

Tears came to his eyes as he said, "You know, I have voted against allowing the Mormon Church on the reservation every time I've had the opportunity. I'll never do that again! Now I'm going to vote for the Mormons to do anything they like on the reservation."

Like a light it hit me why I had been told to start the nursery. I had thought that my work was to provide a healthy environment for those babies so that so many of them would not sicken or die, and then perhaps their parents would be more receptive to the gospel. I'm sure this was part of the plan, but the missionary work on the reservation had been in jeopardy because some of the tribal leaders were in favor of expelling the Mormon missionaries from the reservation. Now the missionaries would be welcome and the children could attend school—just because we had started the nursery!

From that time on, the missionary work among the Lamanites in that area went forth and progressed in an almost miraculous manner. The Indians began to welcome the missionaries into their dwellings, and before long many of these choice Lamanite brothers and sisters were baptized into the Church.

I loved the Lamanite people and had been willing to do anything that would open the way for preaching the gospel to them— except the one thing that the Lord had asked me to do. Never again will I consciously counsel the Lord on how he can best further the work of the kingdom. And, hopefully, in the future I will always listen to the promptings of the Holy Ghost, and obey that still small voice.

BLESSED THROUGH OBEDIENCE

Maria Krolikowska

The Lord has always been there to bless me when I have needed him. He has never failed to help me with my problems, which have been complicated and numerous since my decision to leave my native land of Poland and embrace the gospel. I have received so many blessings from the Lord that it would be impossible for me to ever begin to adequately repay him for all that he has done for me. One thing I could do that might express my deep gratitude and appreciation for his loving care would be to serve him by sharing my testimony and the gospel with those that have not been as blessed as I have. This I did by serving as a missionary in the Alaska British-Columbia Mission for eighteen months.

My mission ended in August of 1973, but it was my desire that this not be the end of my service to the Lord and to my fellowmen. To further this desire, I decided to seek further academic training to prepare for a career in nursing. Accordingly, while I was still on my mission, I applied to Brigham Young University for admittance and was accepted.

Inasmuch as my legal status was that of a Canadian immigrant, it was necessary for me to have a visa to enter the United States. My passport from Poland to England had expired two years earlier, but no one at the immigration office in Vancouver seemed to be concerned about it because I had an insert in my passport stating that I had immigrated from England to Canada. I received a regular student visa for the United States, and therefore assumed that all my papers, including my passport, had to be in order.

With a period of just three days between the time I was released from my missionary labors and the day that my classes were to begin at Brigham Young University, and being short of both time and money, I decided against returning to Canada and took a plane directly to the United States. After landing in Seattle and undergoing the routine check of passports required of all foreigners entering the country, I was informed that my passport was not valid, even with the attached student visa, and that I would not be permitted to remain in the country. However, after much conversation and coaxing on my part, it was finally agreed that I would be allowed to proceed on my way to BYU, providing that

I contact the immigration authorities in Salt Lake City within three days and satisfactorily resolved the matter of my invalid passport.

Two days later I was successfully enrolled at BYU, taking a heavy load of prerequisite classes to qualify for admission to BYU's College of Nursing. I was rather shocked to find out how competitive the nursing program was—out of the three hundred students that would be applying that spring semester, only ninety would be accepted!

The next day, as required, I presented myself before the immigration officer in Salt Lake City. After reviewing my situation, he stated that there were only two possible solutions to the problem of validating expired passports: receiving a Passport Waiver, or obtaining a Certificate of Identity, which, in my case, was the *only* solution that could be considered. I was not familiar with the particulars of either a Passport Waiver or a Certificate of Identity, so I inquired as to what would be involved for me to obtain the certificate.

He replied that I would have to contact the Canadian authorities for accurate information on how to obtain a Canadian Certificate of Identity. I then wrote to the proper Canadian government office and they replied that I would have to *return* to Canada and apply for the certificate in person. I was also advised that there would be a wait of at least two or three weeks for my papers to be processed.

Hoping to avoid returning to Canada just to validate my passport, I consulted the foreign student advisor at BYU. He advised me to withdraw from all my classes, return to Canada and settle the matter with my passport, then return to BYU the next semester. With my financial situation, that would have been very difficult to do.

About this same time I became involved with the Polish Club, which had just been organized that semester. There were twelve members, mostly second and third generation Poles, who wanted to learn the Polish language and work on their genealogy. I was the only member who was actually born in Poland and spoke the language fluently, so I felt a great obligation to help them. This was my first experience of carrying a full class load in an English-speaking university, so my studies were quite demanding. I had to put in more hours studying than did my American roommates, which meant that I wasn't even getting enough sleep. All things considered, I really didn't have the time to become involved with the Polish Club, but I felt that it was my obligation to do so, for I was the only one at the University that could really help them.

To top all this, a counselor in the branch presidency called me in for an interview and asked me to take the position of second counselor in the Relief Society. I replied that I would not be able to accept the call because I was being deported due to passport problems. A short time later I discussed the call with the Relief Society president, who told me that I was the only one they had interviewed for the position. They had prayed for guidance in selecting the counselor and felt very strongly that I was the one the Lord would have called to this position.

This upset me terribly. With my heavy class load and my obligations to the Polish Club, I already had undertaken more than I could comfortably manage. I fully realized the many hours of service that would be required of me if I accepted and properly magnified this calling. I simply did not have the time to give.

I was discouraged and highly distraught as I walked back to my apartment after church that morning. I was so upset that I continued walking after I reached the apartment. For about an hour I walked aimlessly around, crying and pleading with the Lord that somehow he wouldn't put this burden upon me.

I suddenly realized that the Lord had always blessed me when I needed his help, sometimes even performing miracles in my behalf. The Lord had prepared the way for me to accept the gospel and to come to this great University so that I could have a life of serving him and my fellowmen. I had been greatly blessed and if I wished to continue receiving blessings, it would be very wrong for me to decide which of his blessings and responsibilites I would now accept. I cannot accept only those callings and responsibilities that I like, or those that are convenient for me—I must be willing to serve him whenever and however he requires. It seemed to me that unless I was willing to accept both the blessings *and* the responsibilities that the Lord gave to me, the only honorable thing for me to do would be to pack my things and go back to Poland and live without the blessings that had already been given me.

I accepted the calling. I knew it was what the Lord would have me do, and he would somehow help me to fulfill not only that calling, but my other obligations as well. Since I could not fulfill this position if my passport was not validated and I was compelled to return to Canada, I decided to take the problem to the Lord, and began fasting and praying.

I also decided to discuss the matter of the passport once more with the immigration officer in Salt Lake City. I knew that under the circumstances, he probably had no choice but to be obedient to the law and insist on my deportation. Though the most that I could possibly hope for would be a possible extension of a few days, or perhaps even a month, I felt impressed to discuss my passport with him anyway.

Three days earlier, I had received my first American checkbook, which I normally did not carry with me, but this time it was all I took with me to Salt Lake City.

I found the immigration officer in a very amiable mood. He genially asked what he could do to help me. He had completely forgotten about our previous conversation and asked me to review my problem.

I reviewed our earlier discussions, and informed him that I had just received a letter from Ottawa stating that I must return to Canada immediately to start processing my records in order to validate my passport.

"Well," he said exuberantly, "how would you like to pay ten dollars and have me give you a Passport Waiver so that you can stay in the United States without any more problems as long as you continue your studies and do not leave the country?"

Of course I would! I quickly wrote out a check for ten dollars, and hurriedly left without reminding him that only a few days earlier he had rejected the idea of my obtaining a waiver and had insisted that I obtain a Canadian Certificate of Identity, which meant that I *had* to be deported.

A week later I received my Passport Waiver and permission to stay in the United States for another year. The Lord truly opened the way for me to accomplish all that was required of me. I completed my classwork that semester with a GPA of 3.42, which I felt was quite satisfactory for someone studying in a foreign language. I was also able to maintain my association with the Polish Club and received a tremendous satisfaction from helping the members to progress in learning the Polish language and assisting them in applying it in their genealogical research. I was also blessed with the necessary time to fulfill my calling and obligations as a counselor in the Sixty-third Branch Relief Society.

From this experience, I have learned that the Lord will always bless us and open the way to do all that is required of us, *if* we will obediently serve him and do all that he calls us to do in building up the kingdom.

WILL I BE HELD RESPONSIBLE?

Ira Hoyt Heaton

In the spring of 1914 while freighting from Alton (Utah) to Marysvale where we took the wool to be shipped, I took my oldest boy, Reid, with me. He was six years old in April and the next year would have been in school. Bishop Robinson of Kanab passed me in a buggy about five miles from home. As we passed, he said, "Ira, send that boy back; he will get killed." I did not heed the warning as he had gone with me the year before along with twelve other boys with their fathers. They had such fun.

Reid was with me all the time and was a great help and a good companion. We rode all the way to Marysvale on the high load of the wagon. When the wool was shipped, we loaded up some flour that covered the bottom of the double wagon box and started for home.

About six miles north of Panguitch, in front of the Tebbs Ranch, there was a little down grade. I had four horses, the lines in one hand and the brake in the other. I was sitting in the spring seat, Reid was sitting inside the box at my feet, his feet on the dashboard. He had been carving animals with my knife out of clay cakes left along the canyon when the Hatch Town Dam went out and flooded the canyon. He must have gone to sleep completely relaxed, for when the horses started to trot, the jolt of a wheel hitting a rock threw him over the front of the box, his head hit the ground, breaking his neck and the wheel ran over one of his legs and an arm. Dr. Clark of Panguitch was called, but Reid must have died almost instantly.

This was a great shock to me because of the warning of Bishop Robinson and I felt that if I'd left him home he would have lived.

He was such a nice, sweet boy, and I cannot help but wonder if I will be held responsible, after being warned.

> Gwen Heaton Sherratt and Hannah Heaton Roundy, *Esther's Children* (William Heaton Family Organization, 1955), p. 100.

PRAYER

Pray always, and I will pour out my Spirit upon you, and great shall be your blessing—yea, even more than if you should obtain treasures of earth and corruptibleness to the extent thereof.

—*Doctrine and Covenants* 19:38

A PRAYER FROM BEHIND THE IRON CURTAIN
Kiril Kiriakov

My native land of Bulgaria is a beautiful country graced with the majestic Balkan Mountains that traverse the center of the country and many fine resort towns along the Black Sea, but living in Bulgaria is not a beautiful experience. Everything one could desire for living the "good life" was there—except freedom. Not only is Bulgaria behind the iron curtain, but of all the eastern European states, Bulgaria is the one most influenced by Russia.

The Communists have been in power in Bulgaria since 1945 and they control everything. They maintain many powerful organizations which help them to keep the masses of people under firm subjection, and *no one*, no matter how young, escapes their domination. The Communists have even created The League of Young Pioneers, an organization to which all children from ten to fifteen years must belong. Many recreation centers for this youth league have been established, and therein, through the work and games of the children, they may introduce many of the teachings of communism.

The schools, also controlled by the Communist government, have been very effective in their attempt to turn the younger generation from God with their atheistic doctrines. Should this indoctrination fail and one of your children be seen attending church with you, you will then be considered an enemy of communism. Later on you will be unable to get a recommendation for that child's entry into the university.

One soon learns that life will be more comfortable and profitable if one disavows any belief in God and shuns any public worship that would quickly denote less than total dedication to the Communist atheistic way of life. In spite of the rigorous programs and propaganda promoted by the Communists, however, many of the older generation of Bulgarians still *privately* confess a belief in God, or a supreme being.

The circumstances under which the Bulgarians are forced to live causes many of them to long to leave the land of their birth and escape to the free world. Some have tried to escape, but they are either killed in the attempt or are captured and taken to prison where they will spend the rest of their lives behind bars.

In 1963, when Algeria became an independent country, they needed specialists in many occupations in order to increase their economy. Algeria asked Bulgaria for assistance and the Bulgarian government responded by contracting to supply one thousand specialists. Of these, ten were to be dental technicians. At that time, I was working as a dental technician in a state laboratory. When I learned that our lab was to furnish one technician for Algeria, I hoped that I would be the one to go. Though escape from Bulgaria was impossible, there was the remote possibility that I could escape the less tenacious clutches of the Algerian government.

There were seven candidates for the opening and so the possibility of my being chosen was very remote. Most of my colleagues had a contact or a relative who held a high position in the Communist government, someone they could rely on for help. I knew of no one who could help me, so I put my entire faith and hope in our Heavenly Father. My wife and I decided that only our fervent prayers to the Lord could open the door to the free world.

The next day, after many hours of sincere and fervent prayer, I went to work as usual. The climate in the laboratory that day was not one of the usual restraint, but one of nervous excitement over the selection of the technician that would be going to Algeria. A lively conversation was underway as several methods of selecting the fortunate technician were being considered. One of my colleagues proposed that we decide the matter by drawing lots, placing seven folded pieces of paper in a hat, six of which would have the word *no* written on them and one would contain the word *yes*. This seemed to be a fair approach and all agreed that this would be the method used.

The decisive slips of paper with their six no's and one yes were prepared and placed in a hat, with each of us getting progressively more tense and anxious to draw. As my colleagues began withdrawing their slips of paper, my heart was beating so hard that I could barely manage the motor responses necessary to withdraw my slip of paper. When I opened it, I could not believe my eyes. The piece of paper I had drawn had *yes* written on it!

I was overcome with excitement and happiness, but my colleagues were not! They protested the outcome as unfair, since I had been in this laboratory for only eight months while some of the others had been working there for nearly a lifetime. They felt that each of them deserved this choice opportunity much more than I did and insisted that we repeat the drawing. Their objections had some merit, so, with a downcast heart, I reluctantly agreed to submit to another drawing.

We drew our slips of paper from the hat, and *again* I drew the *yes* piece of paper! Again they objected, and this time I had no choice but to comply with their demand for another drawing.

When this same experience was repeated the third time, I was stunned and unable to utter a word! Those about me were also highly surprised, and highly agitated. Some of them simply refused to believe that this was really happening and demanded a fourth drawing. Not knowing what to say and still being in a state of shock, I just nodded my head that I would agree to another drawing.

We drew again. Everyone was trembling as they opened their slips of paper. I opened mine and it said *yes* again. The others grabbed it from my hands and just shook their heads in unbelief.

We repeated the drawing two more times with the same results. By now my colleagues were not only shocked, but also extremely disturbed and becoming openly hostile and angry. Their envy was quite evident, for I suspect I was not the only one in this laboratory hoping to use the position in Algeria as a passport to freedom.

Their anger subsided somewhat and they decided that they would try drawing lots one *last* time. This time, I would not be permitted to take my slip of paper until each of them had drawn their chosen piece of paper. They did not even ask me if I would consent to this procedure; I was simply informed that this was how it would be done.

After the others had drawn their lots and there was only one left in the hat, I was permitted to draw out my slip, which again read *yes*.

This time, instead of objecting in rather strong terms, they marveled that the only way I could draw the *yes* slip seven times in a row would have to be with the help of God! They readily acknowledged that it was a miracle, even though one is not supposed to have religious convictions in Bulgaria.

Several weeks later I received my assignment to Algeria, and after a month and a half my family was permitted to join me. To us the limited freedom of Algeria was like living in a paradise, which only whetted our appetite for the complete freedom to be had only in the free world. As my two-year assignment began to draw to a close, I completed the arrangements to receive permission from the Bulgarian government to return by way of France. My family, however, was required to return directly to Bulgaria, which was the Communist method of discouraging their people from defecting. Then the idea presented itself to add the words *and family* on my exit permit, which we did, and we were then successful in obtaining tourist visas to France for the entire family. Fortunately we lost no time in leaving for Marseilles, for fifteen days after our departure, a bloody *coup d'etat* led by Defense Minister Colonel Boumedienne toppled the Communist-leaning Algerian president, Ahmed Ben Bella. All Bulgarians residing in Algeria were immediately flown home to their country, but we were already in France and had safely defected from our Communist homeland.

About a year later two missionaries of The Church of Jesus Christ of Latter-day Saints came to our home in France and brought us the truths of the restored gospel, something that never would have happened in Bulgaria. I have been deeply impressed that the reason the Lord answered our prayers and helped me to win the drawing to go to Algeria and eventually to the free world was so that my family could have this precious opportunity of finding the true Church.

This choice experience has taught me that God does hear and answer the prayers of all his children everywhere, even those behind the iron curtain in a remote Communist-controlled laboratory.

GOD HAS SENT ME!

Nevenka Kiriakov

When we left our Communist homeland of Bulgaria and defected to the West, we had to make some substantial sacrifices in return for enjoying the precious gift of freedom. Our humble situation as political refugees in France did not permit us to provide for our children all that we would have desired—we had to be content with the necessities of life.

Our daughter Julia had studied English in a special school in Bulgaria and felt confident of her ability to communicate effectively in English. Thus, when she decided that she would like to continue her education at Brigham Young University, the only major consideration was that of finances. I managed to find employment, and each month a portion of my small salary was set aside to finance Julia's education. However, when the time arrived for her to leave we had not accumulated a sufficient sum of money to cover both her travel expenses and tuition. So it was that Julia left for BYU carrying with her only a small amount of money and the promise that I would send the rest of the money for her tuition shortly after her arrival.

An unforeseen event prevented me from keeping that promise to Julia. There simply was not enough work for me to do, so my employer was forced to dispense with my services. There were not enough jobs for everyone in our small town, and because my knowledge of the French language was limited, I was unable to find another position.

In a few days I received a letter from Julia asking about the money I had promised to send. I had neither the money nor the heart to tell her that I didn't even know when I would be able to send her any money, so I didn't answer the letter.

One week later I received a second letter, and in a few days a third letter came stating that she was in dire need of the money for her tuition. I was brokenhearted that I had been unable to keep my promise to my daughter; even worse, I was fearful of the desperate circumstances in which she would soon be placed.

I could no longer evade my responsibilities with the false hope that circumstances would change in the immediate future and I would then be able to earn the money to send to Julia. I had to force myself to cope with the reality that I must set aside my pride and face the embarrassing fact that the *only* way I was going to be able to send Julia the money would be to borrow it.

Several of our neighbors I assumed to be rich—at least in comparison to our humble circumstances they gave the appearance of being exceedingly wealthy. They could easily share of their substance. But would they be willing to risk lending their own money to one with a limited earning capacity and a doubtful future income? I doubted that most of them would, especially since we had been in France only a short time and were not well acquainted in the community. Surely one of them would be willing to assist me when I needed help so desperately, but which one? Being a sensitive person, I hesitated to ask without some kind of assurance that my request would not be rejected. I knew of no one I could turn to for help with my problem except the Lord. A scripture from the New Testament (Acts 1:22-26) came to mind wherein the apostles were faced with the problem of trying to decide which man was the one the Lord desired to have replace the fallen apostle Judas. They appointed two men as being worthy of the calling and then prayed to the Lord for his guidance as to which one should be chosen. They then cast forth their lots and the new apostle of the Lord was chosen without hesitation.

I decided to do the same thing. I appointed five men that I felt would have the means to assist me—two of the brothers from our branch, and three others who were our neighbors. I then kneeled and humbly prayed to my Heavenly Father to show me which one of the five would be a friend and answer my need.

After the prayer, I selected a name—one of our brothers from the branch. Being human, I doubted my judgment as having been inspired and asked the Lord to show me once more which one

I should decide upon. After a fervent prayer I again chose a name—the same name I had chosen before. Again I doubted, thinking that perhaps I was being influenced by the devil. This was my first experience in praying for guidance since we had joined the Church, and I was not sure whether I was being guided by the Lord or deluded by the adversary. I began to tremble, fearful that I was being misguided and was not selecting the man the Lord knew would help me.

Again I kneeled and prayed to my Heavenly Father to please forgive me for doubting and pleaded with him to show me this one last time the name of the man that I should choose. I arose and selected a name, and for the third time, it was the same name. This time I had no doubts, for the Spirit of the Lord rested upon me, testifying that I had made the right choice. Gratefully, and with tears streaming down my face, I bowed my head and thanked the Lord for showing me the way.

I put on my coat and walked to the home of the brother whose name I had chosen each time. He was surprised to see me, and when he inquired as to the reason for my visit, I replied, "God sent me to you!"

He was a very spiritual man and was completely overcome by my statement, so much so that tears came to his eyes and it was only with great difficulty that he was able to respond to my statement. I did not know this man well and I had not realized how tenderhearted and sympathetic he was.

On my way to his home, I had decided to ask him to lend me only half of the money I needed because I really didn't know *his* situation, but the Lord had prepared that man and had guided me to him. When I asked for half the sum I needed he told me that he would not only lend me that amount, but more if I needed it, because the Lord had helped him to earn a very large sum of money that *same* day.

This experience has strengthened my testimony and has shown me that the Lord does watch over his children and minister to their needs, if they will but ask.

The Lord has since helped me many times, and I know he will help me again, because I believe in him.

TEACH THEM THE GOSPEL

Julia Palazuelos

I left my home in Guasave, Mexico, to live with the Lewis family in Gilbert, Arizona, while I was studying and preparing for a career in nursing. I had decided that a nursing career would not only help me to be of service to others, but would also bring me a sense of fulfillment and satisfaction. As time went on, I began to have doubts as to whether I was doing what the Lord would have me do. I was undecided as to whether I should continue my studies in the nursing program at Mesa Community College, transfer to Brigham Young University, or go on a mission. The more I thought about it, the more bewildered I became. A logical analysis of the problem indicated that any of the three choices would be a good one, but which one was *best?* Which one of the choices would be more in keeping with fulfilling my mission in life?

On Thursday, April 4, 1974, I said my prayers as usual and went to bed. My inability to make a decision about my future weighed heavily upon my mind. I was restless and unable to sleep so I got out of bed and read my patriarchal blessing. It occurred to me that perhaps the Lord had already given me the answer in my blessing, but everything I read seemed to be so general. For example: "You are to work with the youth of the Church." That promise could easily be fulfilled no matter which of the three choices I made, and so could all the other blessings that were indicated in my patriarchal blessing. The specific guidance that I had hoped for was not there.

I went back to bed, but I could not go to sleep. I just lay there trying to decide what to do. Suddenly, an overpowering impulse came over me to pray about it, so I got out of bed, knelt down, and fervently asked my Heavenly Father to guide me in making the right choice. I waited, but felt nothing.

I then went back to bed, confused and highly distraught. My patriarchal blessing hadn't been any help, and my Heavenly Father hadn't answered my prayers. I felt rejected, and almost beside myself with anxiety and indecision. I tried to sleep, but that wasn't possible.

The impulse then came to pray again, this time much stronger and more intense than before. Prayer hadn't accomplished anything before, but I couldn't ignore this overpowering feeling. I got out of bed again, knelt down, and started to pray. I poured my heart out to my Heavenly Father and asked for a sure guide as to what I should do with my life. Again and again I pleaded for guidance. Finally, when I returned to my bed, the warmest feeling came into my heart. I no longer felt distraught or confused. My mind seemed to clear and I felt calm and at peace with myself. Suddenly, a personage appeared in my room and I recognized him as Spencer W. Kimball, President of the Church. He appeared not to speak, but the words, "You should go on a mission, because there are so many people waiting for you to teach them the gospel" were strongly imprinted on my mind. In a few moments he was gone, and I was left alone to reflect on this marvelous experience.

My prayer was answered! There was no longer any doubt that the Lord's desires were for me to go on a mission.

Since that experience, I have accepted a mission call to return to my country and teach the gospel to the Lamanite people. I know this is what the Lord would have me do, not only because I was told to go on a mission by President Kimball under rather marvelous circumstances, but because many of the young people of my country are waiting for me to bring them the gospel. I know this is so because I've seen their faces in my dreams.

I hadn't really understood my patriarchal blessing when it stated that I was to work with the youth of the Church. Later on perhaps I will work with these young people through the auxiliaries of the Church, but I must go on a mission and convert them first.

THE BEST INSURANCE

Gwen Heaton Sherratt

Our daily family prayer is the best protective insurance in the world. It can guard us against the little unexpected happenings that could cause us great trouble and regret. Because we can't foresee or know when we need this help, it is best to keep ourselves covered at all times by asking God's help and protection every day.

Last fall when our busy family was reduced to two, my young daughter Judie and myself, we rattled around in the big house trying to feel important and unlonely. Some days we didn't see very much of each other because Judie was in college meeting many new and interesting people. Quite often she invited a group of these new acquaintances to our house to partake of a home-away-from-home atmosphere. She did not dream that any of them might not understand our ways or get the wrong impression of her overtures.

One Saturday night I returned home quite late. It was our practice to leave the back door unlatched for the last arrival to get in. Most of the time it was carelessly left unlocked all night. We had had no reason to fear. That night, however, I had a strong premonition to lock the door securely when I entered. I had started on inside to check whether Judie was home when the prompting came again, so I turned around and fastened the screen and locked the door.

I found my daughter sleeping soundly in my bed. She often made herself my bed-partner when she was lonesome or needed to talk something over with her "Mom." I settled myself beside her and was soon asleep.

During the quietest part of the night, I became aware of a voice whispering hoarsely, "Judie! Judie! JUDIE! . . ." At first I vaguely thought it was my own voice and then I wakened enough to realize that the words were coming from some distance away.

I aroused Judie and went into the hall calling, "What is wanted?"

Quite a draft of cold air was coming down the stairs, which was strange, because I knew the windows up there were closed earlier in the evening. I heard a sort of scraping sound above me, and when I stepped into the kitchen and turned on the light, it was 4:00 A.M. Cautiously I started up the steps, fearful of what I would find.

Just then Judie called, "Mom! I saw someone run into the shadow of the pine tree."

Upstairs, I found my sewing machine, which is placed under the hall window, pushed out into the middle of the floor and the window up as far as it would go—about twelve inches. There was no doubt in our minds that our visitor was real and not a ghost. Of course, we were greatly disturbed and slept no more that night. All day Sunday we wondered if we would ever find out who it was.

When Judie went to school on Monday, she was told quite frankly that one of the young fellows who had visited in our home as a friend had gotten drunk and decided to pay her a call. He first tried the front and back doors, but found them locked, so he decided to try getting to her room, which he remembered was on the second floor of the house. A trellis over the back door served as a ladder for him to get up to the upper hall window. He was intent on hoisting himself through it when I was aroused.

Perhaps there was no great danger, but the prospect of handling a strong young man so uncontrolled and misdirected makes me thankful indeed that our prayer insurance was effective in warning me to lock the door that particular January night.

> Gwen Heaton Sherratt and Hannah Heaton Roundy, *Esther's Children* (William Heaton Family Organization, 1955), pp. 128-129.

PRAYER ROCK

Calvin S. Asay

It was a strange day. A few wisps of white stretched across the hot blue sky like an omen. Through the rocks, the wind sang as if in reverence to that strangeness. There had been many days no different than that one, yet something intangible made it seem different.

I wasn't ill, though for a fleeting instant the thought crossed my mind. "Just lack of sleep," I rationalized aloud. Sleep had been evasive the night before as worry claimed my thoughts. The men were in danger. Proud and defiant, the rock towered at an angle over them. It could fall without warning and crush the life from their strong, agile bodies.

"Byron. Byron Sessions!" someone called from the hole. Troubles had been plentiful from the time construction began on the canal. The ground was much harder than we had anticipated, and our crude tools left much to be desired. It seemed that each new day brought many new problems.

"What's the trouble?"

"We're starting to hit rock about ten feet down."

"Keep at it, men. Bert, you and a couple of other fellas take the picks and hammers and try to break up some of the big ones for the scrapers. The Lord is with us. We'll move this rock," I added.

The three scrapers, somewhat in retirement until the rock in the hole was broken up, created a cloud of dust as they moved away. When the dust cleared, I could see that the hole beside the rock now exposed about twenty feet of the solid gray mass. If we were lucky, the hole was going to weaken the rock so that a shot in its crevice would knock it into the hole, leaving the canal site free.

Sidon Canal, as it was called, held the future of the valley in its digging. Parched land stretched for miles and miles in every direction. Parched, arid land—yes, but add life-giving water to it and it would grow almost anything. We knew this, and the Big Horn Valley, Wyoming, colonization effort, inspired by President Lorenzo Snow and Apostle A. O. Woodruff, was staking its life on it.

"Pull her away," shouted one of the boys working in the hole. The slip-scrapers, again in use, began scraping more bits of earth and rock from the slanting hole. The work was slow and hard under the shadow of the massive stone.

I knew that rock well. For several nights I had knelt alone at its base and prayed to my Father in heaven that we would find a way to move it without harm to the men. By moonlight, its shadow was awesome. It became a challenge to my faith and to that of the Saints.

In the daytime, I studied the rock carefully, searching for a weakness. From a ledge nearby, I saw the sun glisten off it. From a distance, it pierced the air sharply. From on top, I felt the strength that held it fast. It was a stumbling block in my hopes, yet I was sure the Lord would provide a way to bypass it.

"Okay, men, let's take a break," shouted Dave Robertson, the work boss, wiping his brow. "Water the horses, Joe."

I watched as the men moved to the shade. I hadn't known most of them until just a few months earlier. They had come from all walks of life around Utah. I had enjoyed a rather prosperous life myself as the manager, partner, and stockholder in a large land and livestock company. When I received the call from President Snow to supervise the construction of the canal in the Big Horn Basin, I sold all I could to prepare my family to go to the valley.

So, in the year 1900, we found ourselves starting from scratch in the Wyoming wilderness. Life was a struggle in the valley, with no conveniences at all. Many times, as we thought of the things we had left behind in the rapidly progressing state of Utah, it would have been easy to give way to discouragement, but we remembered the work we had been called to do, the love of the Lord, and the blessings to come to this land.

I stood up and looked out at the rock. I felt weak. Behind a small rise I found a place secluded from the conversations of the men. I knelt in prayer.

"Father in heaven," I started, "I humbly kneel before thee to thank thee for this fertile land and for the rich opportunity which lies here. We, a few of thy servants, strive to establish this land unto thee and to build a place in which thy children may live in peace, raise their families, and carry on thy work. We have met a barrier that has stopped our progress. A huge rock is in the path of the canal. For several days we have worked to move it, but it seems humanly impossible. Father, each day we have called upon thee to guide us in this work, and we feel thy closeness. We have faith in thee, and once again I humbly ask thee to grant us this special blessing. Please direct us in the manner by which we can overcome this obstacle. I ask thee also to protect the men from harm. Help me to be ever mindful of that responsibility I bear in watching over them. I thank thee for the many blessings thou hast bestowed upon us and ask for those of which we stand in need, in the name of Jesus Christ. Amen."

I arose from my knees with tears in my eyes. An intense feeling of enlightenment filled every fiber of my being. I stood for a moment looking at the sullen landscape; then it struck me hard again. I ran over the rise and back to the men. They had just started back to work.

"Come back!" I shouted. "You men in the hole—come up here and rest!"

"But we just had a break, Brother Sessions."

"Yes, I know. But come away! Now!"

I knew that they thought I was giving them another break because of the extremely warm weather and also because the horses were weak from lack of good nourishment.

As the men climbed out of the hole and moved away from the rock, I stood for a moment in unspeakable wonder at the feeling in the air, in the men, in the very ground on which I stood. It was beyond description, for it was something much greater than myself.

As the last man walked away from the hole, the answer came like a bolt of lightning. Without a single charge of gun powder, without a single tap of a hammer, without a single pull of a rope, an unusual cracking, splitting sound cut the air. I stood in amazement. The men, wide-eyed, stood frozen.

"The Lord works in mysterious ways," I uttered reverently. We were witnessing a miracle, a direct answer to prayer. The rock split in two, leaving room between for the canal to be built.

When all was silent and the air clear, we knelt and gave thanks to our Father in heaven.

Improvement Era, February 1969, pp. 44-46. Account written from the family records of Byron Sessions.

WILL THE SAINTS TAKE THEM INTO THEIR HOMES?

Golden R. Buchanan

In 1947, I was operating a feed mill in Richfield, Utah, while serving as a member of the Sevier Stake presidency. My calling in the stake presidency committed me to the well-being of all of my Heavenly Father's children residing in the stake, and that included the large numbers of Navajo Indians that had migrated to Sevier County to work in the beet fields. After I had made several trips to their camps to inquire as to their welfare, I became quite concerned over their mistreatment. Some of the Indians were not fortunate enough to have even so much as a tent in which to live, and far too frequently I found that they didn't always have enough to eat.

The living conditions of these Lamanite brothers and sisters were deplorable and heartbreaking. I was determined that something had to be done to change their unfortunate condition. So, as "I stood at the pulpit at the next stake conference, I scolded the members for mistreating the Indians"[1] and admonished them that they had a responsibility to see to the welfare of their employees. Following the conference, however, I was informed by many of the farmers that "the way they treated their employees wasn't a Church matter and the subject had no business being discussed in Church, but I didn't believe that."[2] I felt quite depressed and frustrated over my inability to improve the lot of the Indians, but I didn't know what else to do.

A few days later one of the members of my stake, Amy Avery, came to me with a problem. She told me that a seventeen-year-old Indian girl had refused to return to the reservation with her parents for the winter and had asked to pitch a tent in the Avery back yard. "She wants to live in that tent during the winter and go to school with my daughters," Sister Avery said. "What can I do?" she asked. "I have three daughters of my own to care for."

I rode over to the Avery farm to talk with the Indian girl. When I arrived, I found three Indian girls out in the fields in a snowstorm digging out the remaining beets that were frozen in the snow. They were covered with mud from the waist down and were a pitiful sight to behold. I have never felt sorrier for human beings in my life than when I saw those three teenage girls working in the beet fields with mud and snow almost up to their knees. The three of them had been living way out in the field in six to eight inches of snow in a tent that was about to fall down.

Sister Avery introduced me to the girls and we began to discuss their situation. "I'm going to stay," said Helen John. "I am not going home. I want to get an education."

My heart and admiration went out to her. As I began to think about her plight and her desires for an education, I began to realize what a tremendous thing it would be for this girl, and all the other Indian children who so desired, to receive an education. But how?

As I began thinking and praying for guidance and inspiration, it was as if the whole program opened up to my understanding. I recognized what could be done for our Indian brothers and

---

[1]*Church News*, January 1, 1972, p. 5.
[2]Ibid.

sisters, and I also understood what it could do for our missionary work among the Indians.

"But," I asked myself, "will our Saints take them into their homes?" The answer came back, "Yes, by the thousands!"

I had the answer, but I needed to share it with someone who was in a position to implement the program within the Church. I finally had the temerity to write to Elder Spencer W. Kimball, outlining a program for bringing Helen John and the others like her into the homes of the Church members so these young Indians could get an education.

Two days later, about eight o'clock in the evening, our doorbell rang. The gentleman at the door introduced himself as "Brother Kimball of Salt Lake City."

After dinner, Elder Kimball and my family gathered in the living room to discuss the letter I had written. Elder Kimball brought up the idea of the placement of the Indian youth in the homes of our members and then turned to my wife and asked if she would take Helen into our home as a daughter.

"Oh, I couldn't do that!" she replied. "The neighbors wouldn't like me and would talk about me."

Our sons also indicated that they had some reservations about taking an Indian into our family.

Elder Kimball then asked us if we would consider the matter through the night and then see how we felt about it.

The next morning, our hearts were softened. Our son, a senior in high school, said, "Mother, when a prophet of the Lord asks you, you can't say no. I am willing to take the kidding I'll get at school."

We agreed to take Helen into our family and the two other girls were also placed in good LDS homes. Thus, the Indian Student Placement program began, and, just as I had been told, the Saints have taken these young Indian students into their homes, by the thousands.

UNITED IN FAITH AND CLEAR OF SIN

When Elder Abel Evans was crossing the Atlantic in charge of a company of Saints emigrating to Utah, a terrible epidemic in the nature of a fever broke out on the ship, and threatened the destruction of all on board.

He felt that their only hope lay in securing the favor of the Almighty, and determined to muster all the faith he could in appealing to the Lord. He called together four elders of experience who were on board, and asked them to retire with him to the hold of the vessel and unite in prayer.

They did so again and again without any apparent good result, and Brother Evans marveled at the cause. It was such an unusual thing for him to fail to have his prayers answered that he was surprised that it should be so in that instance, and he could only account for it by lack of union or worthiness on the part of the elders.

He therefore called the four elders again to retire with him to the hold of the ship, and took with him a basin of clean water. When they had reached a secluded place where they were not likely to be overheard or disturbed by others, he talked to the elders about the necessity of their being united in faith and clear of sin before God if they desired to call upon him and receive a blessing. "Now," he said, "I want each of you elders who feels that his conscience is clear before God, who has committed no sin to debar him from the enjoyment of the Holy Spirit, and who has faith in the Lord Jesus Christ sufficient to call upon the Almighty in his name and claim the desired blessing to wash his hands in that basin."

Three of the elders stepped forward and did so; the fourth could not—his conscience smote him. He was therefore asked kindly to retire, and the four others joined in earnest prayer before the Lord and rebuked the disease by which the people were afflicted. The result was that the epidemic ceased its ravages and the sick recovered from that very hour, much to the surprise of the ship officers and others on board who knew nothing of the power by which such a happy result was accomplished.

"Scenes in the British Mission," *Early Scenes in Church History* (Eighth book of the Faith-Promoting Series, Salt Lake City: Juvenile Instructor Office, 1882), p. 40.

AN ANSWER TO PRAYER

In the days when John Morgan was president of the mission, it was customary for the missionaries to travel without purse or scrip and to rely upon the hospitality and generosity of the people of the country to whom they were preaching and teaching the principles of the gospel. On one occasion when President Morgan was holding a council meeting with a group of traveling missionaries in the backwoods of Tennessee, a number of elders had reported very poor results in interesting the people. In an endeavor to ascertain the reason for this lack of interest on the part of the people, President Morgan inquired of the elders reporting negligible results if they had sufficient money to purchase the food they had needed and lodging whenever it was necessary. The elders stated that they had; that they had never missed a meal and that they had been paying regularly for their lodging. So far as their travels were concerned, they were enjoying themselves greatly. The following morning, President Morgan directed Elder James Ford of Centerville, Utah, and his companion, two of the elders reporting unsatisfactory results, to start on their journey by foot to a hitherto unvisited section of the country and to travel without purse or scrip.

Here is a story of pathos. It was early when they started. They had walked briskly until dark without meeting anyone or seeing any habitation where food or lodging might be obtained. Nevertheless they continued on their journey. Shortly after dusk, very dark clouds developed in the sky and there was a great deal of thunder and lightning. The two missionaries quickened their pace but still the entire countryside seemed uninhabited. It started to rain, lightly at first, and then very heavily.

Coming to a trail that led through some heavy timbers, they left the main road and hurried to the shelter of the trees. The rain rapidly developed into a torrent and the elders were soon drenched to the skin. It grew desperately dark. The trail through the trees was a heavy one—sticky clay—making it most difficult to travel. Tired, hungry and cold, they stopped to rest. The rain had ceased, but they did not know where they were or what to do. In that moment, Elder Ford's companion, trembling with cold and emotion, suggested that they kneel on the damp ground and pray; that President Morgan had promised them divine aid should circumstance require it.

Surely they had done their duty and were willing and desirous of carrying on. Surely God would hear and answer their prayer. Then, on bended knees, far from home and loved ones, lost in what they thought was a wholly uninhabited country in the cold and dampness of the woods, the two young elders knelt in prayer. Elder Ford did the praying. He had prayed daily since he was a boy at his mother's knee, but never until now had he known the true meaning and power of prayer. He talked to the Lord as though he was very near and pleaded for the help necessary to assist them out of their miserable dilemma; and as he prayed, they felt a divine influence about them, and in that moment of supplication they received assurance that the Lord would help them to security and peace of mind. In closing his prayer, Elder Ford, in deep humility, thanked their Heavenly Father for his blessings and for his Spirit which had enlightened their minds and assured them the security for which they prayed.

They arose to their feet and scarcely had risen when they heard measured footbeats as though a horse was approaching; then through the darkness of the night, they saw the flickering light of a lantern through the trees and they knew that someone was approaching. Not knowing what else to do, they stood still until the man with a lantern, astride his horse, rode up to them. "What are you boys doing here?" the stranger asked. "We are lost," the elders replied, "but we are very happy to see you." The man dismounted. "Well," said he, "you boys are in pretty bad shape; you better climb onto this horse and I will lead you back to my house. I went to bed pretty tired tonight and I just couldn't go to sleep. I tossed and turned in bed with a constantly growing feeling that someone out here needed help. I don't know why I did it, but I got out of a nice warm bed and came out into the rain and cold and through these woods because I felt that someone was in trouble. I guess it was you boys who just wouldn't let me go to sleep." Astride the horse, the elders felt the warmth of the animal's body and in their hearts was deep gratitude for their miraculous escape.

Bryant S. Hinckley, *The Faith of Our Pioneer Fathers* (Salt Lake City: Bookcraft Publishers, n.d.), pp. 252-254.

PROTECTION

Undoubtedly angels often guard us from accidents and harm, from temptation and sin. They may properly be spoken of as guardian angels. Many people have borne and may bear testimony to the guidance and protection that they have received from sources beyond their natural vision. Without the help that we receive from the constant presence of the Holy Spirit, and possibly from holy angels, the difficulties of life would be greatly multiplied.

—John A. Widtsoe, *Gospel Interpretations,* pp. 28-29

WARNINGS OF THE SPIRIT
H. G. B.

There are no people on the earth that we are acquainted with that exercise so much faith in God our Heavenly Father as do the Latter-day Saints. No other people seek for his protecting care as they do. Nor are there any people to whom his protection is oftener extended or made manifest more visibly than unto this people.

Especially has this been the case with hundreds of our elders when traveling and preaching the gospel. A few of these instances of divine protection in my own experience I wish to relate.

While on my way to Nauvoo, Illinois, in the month of June, 1845, going down the Ohio River, the steamer I was aboard ran aground on the Flint Island Bar just above Evansville, Indiana.

I remained on the boat for thirty-six hours, when, the water in the river being very low and getting lower every day, and, seeing no prospect of our getting past this bar, I concluded to go ashore and work a few days, as I understood laborers were in demand in

Evansville. The captain of the steamer aground accordingly refunded me a just proportion of the passage money I had paid him.

I procured work for one week, at the end of which time the river began to rise. Being very anxious to pursue my journey, I went aboard the first boat that landed at Evansville, which I learned was going as far up the Mississippi River as Galena. I made arrangements with the clerk for passage to Nauvoo, but did not pay him at the time, as he said the boat would not leave for two hours.

I was never more desirous of pursuing my journey than I was on this occasion, yet soon after going aboard a feeling of aversion to going on that steamer took possession of me. Instead of a sensation of joy, an undefinable dread or foreboding of coming evil was exercising an influence over me that increased in its power every moment until I could resist no longer, and, snatching up my trunk, I fled with it to shore just as the deck hands stopped to haul in the gangway, and the boat moved off.

I put my trunk down on the bank of the river and sat down on it, too weak to stand on my feet longer.

This was a new experience to me then. What did it mean? One thing was certain, I felt as if I had just escaped from some great calamity to a place of safety.

Two days after this I took passage on another steamer for St. Louis, where in due time I arrived in safety. As I walked ashore I met a newsboy crying his morning paper, and among the items of news it contained, the most prominent was an account of the ill-fated steamer that I had made my escape from at Evansville, on the Ohio River. I purchased the paper, and found the boat had been snagged in the Mississippi River, below St. Louis, in the night, and sank with a loss of nearly all that were on board.

The mysterious feeling that impelled me to leave that boat was cleared up to my satisfaction. There remained not the shadow of a doubt that Providence had interposed between me and the great danger.

The thanks, gratitude, and joy that filled my whole being on this occasion, I will not try to describe.

Gems for the Young Folks (Fourth book of the Faith-Promoting Series, Salt Lake City: Juvenile Instructor Office, 1881), pp. 22-24.

THE LORD STOOD AT OUR SIDE

M. Douglas Wood

Former President of the West German Mission

I shall never forget the choice privilege I had of associating with the noble missionaries in the West German Mission, and I'm sure those elders will never forget the choice experiences they had in that country, or the difficulty they had in getting out of Germany when World War II broke out.

Friday, August 25, 1939, my wife and I were in Hanover when I received a telegram from the First Presidency informing me that we were to immediately evacuate all the missionaries in Germany and go to either Holland or Denmark.

Everything had been so peaceful only a few hours earlier, but it rapidly became quite clear that in a few short hours peace was going to be only a precious memory. Hanover suddenly became a city of women—all the men had been mobilized into the German Army that was swelling its ranks to awesome proportions. Women, who were assuming the positions that the men vacated as they left for war, were even operating the street cars. There was a feeling of excitement in the air as everyone scurried about trying to prepare for what was soon to come.

Things were happening fast—perhaps too fast for me to get all our missionaries out of the country before it was too late. I knew there probably wouldn't be enough time for me to continue our leisurely drive into Frankfurt and the mission headquarters, so I went to the hotel clerk and asked him to get me two reservations on the next plane to Frankfurt. "I don't think that will be possible, sir," he replied. "I'm sure that all reservations have been taken for some time. Frankfurt is on the main European line and those reservations are usually gone two weeks in advance. And now with this Polish trouble, I'm sure you could not buy a ticket for *any* consideration!"

"Please call anyway," I urged. "I *must* have two tickets."

"Well, if you insist," he said. "But, it won't do any good."

He made the phone call and with a very perplexed look on his face answered, "There are two tickets left."

"That's all we need," I replied.

An hour and twenty minutes later we arrived in Frankfurt. We were on the last passenger flight that plane made before it was sent to the Polish front.

We made contact with the Dutch consul in Frankfurt and received permission for the missionaries to enter Holland, providing they also had tickets for London in their possession and would remain in Holland only a relatively short time. I knew that getting those missionaries into Holland was not going to be an easy task. We had eighty-five elders scattered from the Danish border on the north to Vienna on the south, which covers considerable distance. We immediately sent telegrams to all of the elders telling them to cross over into Holland that night and to telephone or telegraph the office as they left so we could check on them.

That afternoon and evening we sat in the office and waited for telephone calls, but the phone didn't ring. We then tried to check on the missionaries by phoning them, but we were unable to get through because the lines were jammed. We tried sending more telegrams to the elders, but we were told that they were no longer sending telegrams.

Early Saturday morning one of the elders called us by telephone from the Dutch border. He and his companion had been there for six hours and the Dutch would not let them in. The Dutch authorities had remembered the last war and the lack of food in their country, so they were determined not to let *any* foreigners into their country. Things were happening so fast that this new policy had not been communicated to the Dutch consul in Frankfurt. The Germans had a controlled currency and would not allow any German marks to leave the country. Since the elders were aware of this, they had given all of their German money to the local Saints when they departed for the Dutch border. "The Dutch won't let us in and we don't have a mark between us," the missionary said. "What do we do?"

"I'll get some money to you somehow so that you can go to Denmark," I replied. "Just have faith, Elder!"

I phoned the telegraph office and arranged to send the money to those two elders. A few minutes later the operator called me back and said, "We will not be able to take any more money by telegraph; however, I think I can get this last one through."

About that time a radio announcement was made by the government that after midnight on Sunday the German government would not guarantee anyone his destination on the railways. I shall never forget our feelings at that time. Neither telephone nor telegraph facilities were available to us, and the railways would be operating for only a few more hours. We were unable to contact our missionaries and we knew that most of them would be heading for Holland and would arrive without money to purchase tickets to Denmark.

Time was against us. We knew that the elders would have to be safely out of the country within the next few hours if we were to avoid the fate of the elders that were trapped in the country during the last world war. Some of the missionaries had to crawl on their hands and knees and make their way out behind the Russian lines. One elder never did make it out of the country and had to remain for the duration of the war.

About this time, a big football-playing elder from Idaho, who weighed over two hundred pounds, came into our office.

"Elder, have you ever carried a message to 'Garcia'?" I asked.

"No," he replied, "but I'm willing to try."

"Elder," I said, "we have thirty-one missionaries lost somewhere between here and the Dutch border. It will be your mission to find them and see that they get out."

He set out with five hundred marks and tickets for Denmark. The only instructions we could give him were to follow his impressions, for we had no idea which towns those thirty-one elders were in now.

After about four hours on the train, he arrived in Cologne, which was about halfway to the Dutch border. Cologne was not his destination, but he felt impressed to get off the train. The Cologne station is one of the largest in Germany and was filled with thousands of people. The call to arms had been given that day and the station was crowded with thousands of servicemen on their way to the Polish border. Hundreds of students returning to England and people prematurely returning from vacations jammed into the station. It was next to impossible to find anyone in that facility. Our football-playing elder stepped into the overcrowded station and began whistling our missionary theme—"Do What Is Right, Let the Consequence Follow."

Down in one corner of that station was a missionary, with an elderly couple who were also serving as missionaries. They heard the call and made their way through the crowd to our ticket-carrying elder. They had been stranded in that depot all day without anything to eat, unable to phone for help.

They boarded the train and continued on their way to the border, with the elder from Idaho getting off whenever he felt impressed to do so, gathering up missionaries along the way. At some stations he felt no impression at all, so he did not get off the train.

When he arrived at the border, he found eight missionaries who had been locked up in the station house all night. Were they glad to see the missionary from the mission office, those tickets to Denmark, and the money! A border official who also noticed the obviously large sum of money stepped up and asked the elder how much money he had.

"Five hundred marks," was the reply.

"Give me that money!" the officer demanded.

"I will over my dead body!" was the missionary's answer. "I was sent here to help these missionaries and I will not give up this money."

Just at that time, a man in a far corner of the station was placed under arrest for being a spy. A spy being apprehended at the border during wartime is quite an exciting occurrence, so it attracted everyone's attention. The moment the border officer turned his head to observe this event the elders stooped down and furtively made their way out of the station and onto the train.

I had previously informed President Murdock of the Dutch Mission that a number of our missionaries would be arriving in Holland by way of Oldenzaal, a tiny village on the eastern border of Holland, which was not more than seven kilometers from the German city of Bentheim. Six elders had crossed the border into Holland late on the night of the twenty-sixth, but had been hurried back into Germany after having been emphatically refused entry into Holland. President Murdock had arranged for Elder Kest to go to Oldenzaal with sufficient funds to conduct the missionaries from Oldenzaal to the mission home in Holland. He had assumed that the elders had been refused entry because of a lack of funds and not having tickets to England in their possession.

Elder Kest states: "I was carrying enough money to assure those cautious border officers that our missionaries would in no way be a burden to the Dutch government while they were in Holland, and I would guarantee their passage into England. I boarded the train for Oldenzaal and there were innumerable delays. The train trip, which could usually be made in two hours, took well over four, and it was after 11:00 A.M. when the train finally arrived in Oldenzaal. The station master, a portly fellow whose fantastic English phrases made me smile, proved very helpful. 'Yes,' he said, 'a number of young American missionaries were sent back to Germany late last night and have not crossed back into Oldenzaal since.' This was upsetting news, for we had fully expected the brethren to be waiting at Oldenzaal, needing only money and an assurance of transportation to England in order for the Dutch authorities to consent to their passage to The Hague. Even after the phone call President Murdock had received the previous evening, we thought the elders had been delayed by some triviality—probably minor border regulations. Already a good twelve hours had elapsed since they had been returned to Germany; something must be *very wrong* indeed.

"Attempting to call Bentheim in order to learn the where-abouts of the elders proved of little value and after three hours I gave up the job as hopeless. Telephone connections with Germany had been cut off. (Afterwards it was found that the elders in Bentheim had been trying to call The Hague for hours, likewise without success.)

"I phoned President Murdock in The Hague along about 2:30 P.M. and told him that it had not been possible to contact the elders; all attempts at phoning them had proved fruitless; it was impossible to contact Bentheim by phone. The station master told me the young men had been almost without funds and had nothing except cameras to declare at the Dutch border. It was obvious that they had no tickets in their possession and probably scarcely enough money to adequately take care of their needs. Therefore, the fact that they were obliged to return to Bentheim began to assume serious proportions. President Murdock had said the elders must be helped at any cost. 'Do your best and use your judgment as to what should be done, Elder Kest.' This advice that President Murdock had given me kept repeating itself in my mind. But what should be done at the moment?

"President Murdock's decision to have me go to the border had been made in such haste that there had naturally not been time to obtain a visa, which would have legally enabled me to enter

Germany. In fact, at the time no one thought such a move would be necessary. For an hour I phoned The Hague, the American consulate, the Dutch embassy, asking if a visa might not somehow be arranged. They all said it was impossible. Hundreds of phone calls had been pouring in begging them to take care of stranded Americans and other Europeans who were desperately attempting to get out of Holland, and some of whom were begging help to extricate relatives and loved ones from Germany. It was impossible to handle the sudden abnormal volume. Their office forces had been working sixteen to eighteen hours straight; no help could possibly be given me.

"After thoroughly discussing the matter with the station master and finding that under no circumstances would they allow the brethren to enter Holland, it became apparent that I must go into Germany, visa or no visa.

"President Murdock had given me something over three hundred guilders; it was thought this amount would take care of any eventuality which might arise. It took almost this entire amount to purchase ten tickets from Oldenzaal to Copenhagen, Denmark. President Wood had said only the night before that many missionaries had been pouring into Denmark, so it was reasonable to suppose the border there would still be open.

"The 2:30 train sped on toward Bentheim. Why the Dutch authorities allowed me to board that train, never asking for a visa, is a mystery; it was most irregular. Sitting tense and excited on the hard seats, the thought reoccurred again and again: 'Is this the right thing to do?' Here I was, speeding into Germany without a visa, under circumstances that were hardly promising, hoping somehow the brethren might still be there. The train stopped; we had arrived.

"A moment later there was a sharp clicking of heels. German Blackshirts stepped quickly through the car, their eyes cold as steel, taking in at a glance the occupants of each car. Handing the leader my passport, the inevitable question was shot at me: 'Why is no visa stamped on the proper page?' The thought suddenly flashed through my mind: 'Brother Kest, you have always enjoyed acting. If you have ever acted a part well, do it now!'

"I explained in exasperatingly slow and deliberately incoherent English that at the present I was living in Holland and heard that some of my friends were in Bentheim and knowing that railroad and train transportation was being curtailed, wanted to visit them while possible. Suspicion shone from the cold eyes of the officers. I rambled on, deliberately, on utterly pointless tangents, hoping all the while they would have great difficulty understanding me, which they did.

"Suddenly, curtly came the question: 'Can you speak no Dutch? No German?'

" 'No,' I replied. 'I've been here a comparatively short while and have not learned the languages well. A few simple phrases I can understand—nothing more.' It was fortunate that the German officer in charge spoke rather poor English. As I went on, talking disjointedly, tossing in a Dutch or German phrase here and there, the effect I wished to produce took hold of the men. They must have concluded that here was a simple, foolish American trying to see some friends for no good reason.

"Inside the little cubicle in the station where they had taken me for questioning, they searched me thoroughly. What would they do to the precious tickets which I had in my suit pocket? This thought was paramount. In my possession was a folder of MIA lessons written in English which we were translating into Dutch to be used the coming winter season. These they read over thoroughly, finally deciding they were harmless. They confiscated binder, papers, passport, *all* the money on my person, and started going through each pocket in both coat and vest. I took the ten tickets out of my pocket and placed them on the table before me. No one seemed to *see* the tickets. The officer in charge gave me a receipt for the money, binder, papers and all my personal effects, and said, 'You have forty minutes to catch the return train to Holland. After that time we cannot guarantee your safety.'

"Taking the tickets from the table, I stuffed them in my pocket. *Not an eye flickered.* I had the strong impression that the action had been entirely unobserved. Hurriedly I left the station, my knees weak, my palms sweating.

"Few people on the street seemed to know where any American boys were staying, but finally someone directed me to the Hotel Kaiserhoff. There the elders were, trying to determine what course they should follow, as they were almost out of money and could no longer afford a hotel bill. After quiet introductions and firm handshaking, my message was quickly delivered. Giving the tickets to Elder Ellis Rasmussen, who seemed to be in charge of the group, I told them quickly that these tickets from Holland might, with luck, insure their passage to Copenhagen. 'You must leave immediately, brethren, and try to make connections into Denmark, as all railroad transportation is being cut off at an alarming rate!' The elders needed no urging, and in less than five minutes were ready, having very little luggage with them.

"Quickly kneeling down, we held a prayer circle and asked our Father that we might be safely conducted to our respective destinations. As the seven of us knelt in fervent prayer, we all felt a closeness and unity experienced very infrequently in life. We were truly united and prayed with power and faith, believing our request would be granted, for we realized the desperate nature of our situation.

"After prayer, we rushed to the station where Elder Rasmussen and his group finally managed to catch a train for Osnabrueck, finally getting to Hamburg and by wonderful circumstances catching an express train to Copenhagen—one of the last out of Germany carrying civilians.

"After the brethren had left, and we waved each other good-bye, I hurried back to the office of the Blackshirts, only a few yards away, where my passport and effects were being held. The station master gave me my money and papers immediately, but a Blackshirt guard stuck my passport in his wide cuff and marched insolently before me as the passengers boarded the train for Holland. The whistle of the train was blowing, and I noted that the clock indicated only three minutes until departure time. What was going to happen? Finally the Blackshirt strutted over and with a sneer handed me my passport, muttering some deprecatory remark under his breath. He pushed me to the ticket window, where I was obliged to buy a German ticket to Oldenzaal even though my Dutch ticket assured passage to Bentheim and return. It was necessary to run in order to catch the train—the wheels had just begun to turn. I sank into the seat, grateful for the brethren's escape and my own now certain and safe return.

"I know that the hand of the Lord guided me and made it possible to deliver tickets to the elders which subsequently enabled them to escape to Denmark. Surely those German officers would have confiscated the tickets had they seen them, since everything else was taken. It is my sincere testimony that the Lord does watch over his children today even as in days of old."[1]

---

[1]*Improvement Era*, December 1943.

I arrived in Denmark early Monday morning with twenty-one missionaries in our group. Later that morning I received a telegram from President Murdock saying that fourteen of our missionaries had arrived in The Hague. That left only seventeen more to worry about. About two o'clock that afternoon, I received a telegram from the football player stating that seventeen missionaries would be arriving that night.

The Lord was with us and stood at our side. With his help we were able to meet all the difficult situations at hand and safely evacuate all our missionaries only hours before war was officially declared. Our hearts were filled with gratitude and humility.

Preparations were made for the missionaries to leave Denmark and return to the United States. One of our elders was then asked if he was a bit anxious about going home on a freighter that would be guided through the mine-infested waters surroundings Denmark by a German pilot.

"That's child's play after the things we have been through getting out of Germany," he said. "I don't think that the Lord would go to all that trouble if he was going to let us down in the middle of the ocean."

URGED BY AN UNSEEN POWER
Albert E. Hopkinson

On August 20, 1920, about five o'clock in the afternoon, a fire broke out in Utah Fuel Company's number 2 mine at Sunnyside. At that time, I was employed as hoisting engineer and also as timekeeper for the mechanical department.

The men fighting the fire sent word for more hose, pipe, wrenches and pipe fittings. I was the only man available at the time, and, knowing the need of haste, I gathered up the materials and tools and went into the mine to the fire, a distance of three miles from the tipple (building where coal is processed). I stayed in the mine and assisted the men.

About 9:00 P.M., Abe Strate took me along with him to disconnect the hoist and the mine pump from the electric cables.

This work took us into the danger zone. We disconnected the hoist and pump and returned to safety. About one o'clock the following day, the superintendent asked me to go with him to the same place where I had been with Mr. Strate. There was an outlet at the mine hoist, but this had been filled in order to prevent fresh air from coming to the fire. Mr. Ostlund, the superintendent, decided to bring fresh air almost to the scene of the fire that the men might work without helmets. Mr. Ostlund and I were quite a distance from the fire inspecting the water lines. No one in the mine knew we were there, and in the excitement and rush nobody missed us.

We went through some old worked-out places and finally reached two big steel doors, hung ten feet apart for the purpose of circulating fresh air to the working places in the mine and return-ing the foul air to the fan. We passed through these doors and went further into the mine. We had gone about two hundred feet when Mr. Ostlund asked me how I was feeling. I told him my legs felt very heavy and he suggested that we go back. We had retraced our steps about one hundred feet when my legs gave way and I fell, but with help and encouragement from Mr. Ostlund we both managed to reach a point about twenty feet from the steel doors. I realized the danger we were in from foul air, and silently I prayed to my Heavenly Father to help us. I then became uncon-scious and Mr. Ostlund must have dragged me to the doors and pushed the first door open before he fell with his back against the door, holding it open. The next door was about ten feet away. If we could have reached a place between the doors, we would have been safe, but with Mr. Ostlund propping the door open, the smoke from the fire would soon reach and suffocate us.

Two men, John W. Littlejohn and Samuel N. Cowley, had been making an inspection of the mine in an opposite direction from where we were. They had reached a point where lunch had been brought for the men who were fighting the fire. They decided to stop and eat, and then, an unseen power possessed them and urged that they hasten back into the mine. They both took a sandwich and hurried on, going directly to the place where we were both lying unconscious. Pulling the door open, they saw Mr. Ostlund's lamp and gave the alarm. We were both taken out, and after working over us for an hour and a half we were revived and our lives saved.

I know it was the power of the Lord that moved these men to come to our rescue, and my heart is full of thanksgiving and praise to my Heavenly Father for this wonderful blessing.

> Jeremiah Stokes, *Modern Miracles* (Salt Lake City: Bookcraft, 1945), pp. 26-27.

PRESERVED BY PRAYER

George C. Lambert

Brother Jedediah M. Brown, of South Bountiful, is a man of great faith. He feels that he has inherited the gift of faith, for he does not remember the time when he did not possess it. When he is in need of anything, it is just as natural for him to appeal to the Lord therefor as it is to work for it, and he is an industrious man who never fails when possible to combine works with faith.

When he was twenty-three years old he was employed by a cooperative sheep company as superintendent of its three large sheep herds that ranged during the winter on the western Utah desert. One part of his duty was to furnish supplies to the several sheep camps, and for this purpose he made occasional trips to the nearest settlements.

In the early part of January, 1888, he started with a horse team from one of the sheep camps to drive to Grantsville, forty miles distant. His intention was to drive to the settlement the first day, buy his supplies and rest his team during the next day, and return to the sheep camp the third day, and so informed the men at the sheep camp before starting.

Having no load, he drove through the first day without trouble, and secured his load, and, fearing some change in the weather might occur that would hinder his return if he delayed starting, he decided to start back the next morning.

The weather had been mild and thawing, but soon after he started it became terribly cold, and the wagon was so hard to pull because of the wheels breaking through the frozen crust that one of the horses gave out before the journey was half accomplished. He had no matches with which to light a fire, nor bedding with which to keep warm, so he did not dare to camp. His only hope was to keep on traveling. The cold was so intense that he suffered the utmost agony, even while trying to keep his blood in circulation by walking.

He realized that he was in danger of freezing to death, and pleaded with the Lord in earnest prayer to spare him from such a fate. After awhile his pain from freezing grew less, and a feeling of numbness and overpowering disposition to sleep took possession of him. His ideas became confused; he scarcely had will power enough left to urge his team along or exert himself to walk; he frequently stumbled and fell to the ground, and he had great difficulty in regaining his feet; his power to resist the feeling of utter exhaustion and desire to sleep were almost gone.

Just then a man on horseback appeared in sight, and as he drew near he was recognized as Charles A. Howard, one of the men from the sheep camp. It transpired that this man, about the time in the morning when Brother Brown's situation became critical, was very strongly impressed to start out to meet him, although he had no reason to suppose that he would be on the road. He tried to reason away the impression but could not, then failed to act upon it for several hours, until it became so strong that he could resist it no longer, when he mounted a horse and started towards Grantsville, protected to the utmost from the intense cold. His horse was fresh, and he rode as rapidly as possible. He had traveled almost if not quite fifteen miles without seeing a sign of a human being, and was beginning to doubt the wisdom of what seemed to be his fruitless trip when he espied a team in the distance. As he approached nearer he saw that it was his friend, and that his movements were much like those of a drunken man, staggering as he walked. He hastened to him, and found him so far gone that he could scarcely speak. He realized that he would have to act quickly to save his life, and that his only hope lay in taking him to the sheep camp, for Grantsville was so much farther away it would be useless to try to take him back there. It was then almost sunset, and growing more severely cold every minute. He hastily unharnessed the exhausted horse, saddled it and helped the suffering man to mount it, then hitched his riding horse to the wagon in the place of it. Urging Brother Brown to ride as fast as possible, he started driving the team towards the sheep camp. The frozen man, however, couldn't even maintain his seat upon the horse and had to be placed in the wagon, where it was with difficulty he was kept awake by his friend as he almost frantically drove the team.

They had not proceeded more than a mile and a half when, to their surprise, they came upon a sheep camp, which had just located beside the road, and which was nowhere in sight when young Howard had passed the spot going eastward.

The herd belonged to Bishop J. W. Hess, of Farmington, and one of his sons was in charge of it. As he afterwards explained, his camp had been located some distance away and he had no intention of moving it until the afternoon of that day, when, without any reason that he could offer, and notwithstanding the cold weather, he took a sudden notion to do so, and acted upon it. It was providential for Brother Brown that he had done so, as he might not have survived the long ride to his own camp.

A good fire was burning in the stove in the camp wagon, and the frozen man was immediately helped in beside it, and with true western hospitality every comfort the camp afforded was placed at his disposal. Stimulants were immediately supplied him, his boots were cut from his feet, as they could not be otherwise removed, and a proposition was made that his feet be thawed out in the oven of the stove, but young Howard knew that would be unwise, so he sat up all night and kept them packed in snow.

In the afternoon of the following day Brother Brown was removed to his own camp, where he had to remain and be cared for during the ensuing two weeks before he could stand it to ride home. During all that time it was necessary to keep his feet elevated, as the pain in them when hanging down was unbearable.

He never recovered the use of his feet until spring, as the skin peeled off them from his ankles to the ends of his toes, and the nails also were shed. He has always since regarded the help he received from Brothers Howard and Hess as a direct answer to his prayer.

"Elder Brown's Experience," *Gems of Reminiscence,* (Seventh book of the Faith-Promoting Series, Juvenile Instructor Office, 1915), pp. 155-159.

THANKFUL FOR HIS PRESERVING CARE
President Wilford Woodruff

On the sixteenth of November (1835) I preached at Brother Camp's and baptized three. On the day following, it being Sunday, I preached again at Brother Clapp's and baptized five. At the close of the meeting I mounted my horse to ride to Clark's River, in company with Seth Utley, four other brethren and two sisters. The distance was twenty miles.

We came to a stream which was so swollen by rains that we could not cross without swimming our horses. To swim would not be safe for the females, so we went up the stream to find a ford. In the attempt we were overtaken by a severe storm of wind and rain, and lost our way in the darkness and wandered through creeks and mud. But the Lord does not forsake his Saints in any of their troubles. While we were in the woods suffering under the blast of the storm, groping like the blind for the wall, a bright light suddenly shone around us and revealed to us our dangerous situation on the edge of a gulf. The light continued with us until we found the road; we then went on our way rejoicing, though the darkness returned and the rain continued.

We reached Brother Henry Thomas's in safety about nine o'clock at night, having been five hours in the storm and forded streams many times. None of us felt to complain, but were thankful to God for his preserving care.

> Wilford Woodruff, *Leaves from My Journal* (Third book of the Faith-Promoting Series, Salt Lake City: Juvenile Instructor Office, 1882), p. 20.

RESPONSE TO IMPULSE SAVES SMALL BOY

Oscar W. McConkie threw down the newspaper he had been reading and dashed out the kitchen door, leaving his young wife, mouth agape, wondering what had come over him.

He checked himself, wondering why he had been impelled to burst out of the house. At that moment, a riderless horse came thundering out of the apple orchard at full speed. Lawyer McConkie moved quickly to bring the animal to a halt. Only then did he see that his small son Bruce was hanging on the far side of the horse, his foot caught in the stirrup and his hand clutching a thin leather thong attached to the saddle.

Brushed out of the saddle as the frightened horse dashed through the orchard, Bruce had managed to hold onto the thong. That slender leather lace, a firm grip and a father's quick response to impulse saved a future Church leader from serious injury or even death.

Church News, July 31, 1965, p. 16.

WHEN JEHOVAH FIGHTS
President Joseph Smith

[Nearing their destination in Missouri after the long trek from Ohio, Zion's Camp was threatened by a large mob gathering ahead.]

This night [June 19, 1834] we camped on an elevated piece of land between Little and Big Fishing Rivers. About sundown five members of the mob rode into camp, and with many blasphemies said, "You'll see hell before morning!"

When these five men were in our camp, swearing vengeance, the wind, thunder and rising clouds indicated an approaching storm, and in a short time after they left, the rain and hail began to fall. The storm was tremendous. Very little hail fell in our camp, but from half a mile to a mile around, the stones or lumps of ice cut down the crops of corn and vegetation generally, even cutting limbs from trees. The lightning flashed incessantly; the roaring of the thunder was tremendous. The earth trembled and quaked. It seemed as if the mandate of vengeance had gone forth from the God of battles. Our enemies swore that the water rose thirty feet in thirty minutes in the Little Fishing River. They reported that one of their men was killed by lightning and that another had his hand torn off by his horse drawing his hand between the logs of a corn crib while he was holding him on the inside.

About forty of these braggarts, drenched and crestfallen, took the "back track" for Independence to join the main body of the mob, fully satisfied that when Jehovah fights, they would rather be absent.

Joseph Smith, *Documentary History of the Church,* Vol. 2, pp. 103-104.

SACRAMENT

The sacrament of the Lord's Supper is a very important and sacred ordinance; however simple it may appear to our minds, it is one which will add to our acceptance before God or to our condemnation.

—Joseph F. Smith, *Journal of Discourses,*
15:324, February 9, 1873

TRUE TO OUR COVENANTS
Andre K. Anastasion, Sr.

In July, 1937, President Heber J. Grant, who with other Church officials was attending the British Mission centennial conference in Rochdale, Lancashire, made a prophetic statement to the effect that "every missionary from Zion will be removed from the British Isles."

On September 3, 1939, Great Britain declared war against Nazi Germany. By a joint order of the British and United States governments, all U. S. nationals not directly involved in the war were to leave the British Isles. This affected all of our missionaries from the United States.

By the end of 1939 some 130 missionaries had left the shores of England. For the first time in 102 years the British Mission was left without a single missionary from Zion, and the prophecy of President Grant was literally fulfilled within two and a half years.

My two counselors, James P. Hill and James R. Cunningham, and I were set apart by President Hugh B. Brown, the retiring mission president, prior to his departure, and were to assume charge of the British Mission. Our appointment was confirmed by a cable from the First Presidency. I devoted my full time to the mission.

Entrusted with the financial responsibility of the British Mission, I was left a sum of about two hundred pounds sterling (then eight hundred dollars) as mission funds, with the parting advice to go very carefully with the money, because "you may not get any more." From the monthly reports coming in, the tithes and fast offerings were often less than the funds requested by some of the branches, and I was constantly concerned about how to meet our financial obligations. Letters sent to the branch presidencies to encourage members to a more faithful observance of the laws of tithing and fast offerings had not helped us, and I was afraid that our mission reserve would not last long, although we economized in every way possible. I was reluctant to dictate a letter to the headquarters of the Church for financial assistance, bearing in mind the parting advice given me. And to close some branches was unthinkable.

"There must be another way," I thought, "a better way to solve our financial problems together." Then I remembered the counsel of the Lord: "Ask, and ye shall receive; knock, and it shall be opened unto you. . . ."

More and more I asked the Lord in prayer for wisdom. One day after fasting I told my wife that I intended to fast the next day also, as I had much on my mind. She looked at me very concerned and said, "You had better eat tomorrow and fast the next day." I followed my wife's advice and then continued altogether for thirty-five days, fasting every other day. This I did in all humility, having no other reason than to seek the Lord's guidance on how to solve our mission's financial situation.

After concluding my days of fasting and communion, I related to my counselors that during those thirty-five days I had received no impression at all about money—nothing about tithing or fast offerings. The only impression that manifested itself and continued with me was about the sacrament, and I felt the assurance that in this sacred ordinance of the restored gospel lay the answer and solution to our financial problem.

Before our annual district conference, we held an early sacrament and testimony meeting, and again I felt the same impression and assurance. After the bread and water had been blessed and passed to each one of us, I reflected on what we had done in partaking of the sacrament. We had asked our Heavenly Father to bless the bread and water, and we in turn had entered into a covenant to take upon ourselves the name of his Son, to always remember him, and to keep the commandments that he had given us. I asked those present if we had intelligently and conscientiously realized the covenants we had made, or if we had partaken of the sacrament as a matter of procedure. We realized that the answer to this could only be found within the heart and mind of each one personally. I reminded those present of the words of the scriptures that the sacrament would be a curse to those who would partake unworthily, and suggested that each time we partake of the sacrament we should silently, with bowed heads, examine our conduct and our hearts so that we might always be true to our covenants and sacred obligations and manifest an intelligent faith by our works and deeds before the Lord. Thus we might enjoy his blessings.

"None of us would wish to bear false witness. A wilful or careless disregard in failing to return the Lord's 10 percent, obeying the Word of Wisdom, or observing the spirit of the Sabbath would, in my opinion, constitute a false witness on our part. One cannot partake of the sacrament and bear sacred witness to God to follow him and then disregard his instructions," I said.

Then I was led to make this promise: "Your tithes and offerings will be returned to you, multiplied a hundredfold, as your inheritance in Zion, when the Lord shall come again."

The impression gained from my appeal was such that some of our members for a time stopped partaking of the sacrament. They understood. But before long it was our joy to learn that most of the members were again partaking of the sacrament. The branch presidents were advised not to question those who still refrained, but to show them love and kindness, and to visit them often. It was particularly stressed that those who were called to administer the sacrament should repeat the sacrament prayers in a clear voice and pronounce each word distinctly and reverently, for it was a matter of personal witness and covenant between every Latter-day Saint and the Lord.

The British Saints took the appeal to heart, and there was evidence of sustaining faith and effort on their part. The monthly reports coming in were most encouraging, and I was spared the necessity of writing for financial assistance from Church headquarters.

It was almost four and a half years before President Brown was able to return to England and resume the responsibility of the British Mission. By then we had seventy-eight branches and fourteen districts under the local priesthood leadership. Over four hundred local missionaries had labored during the war years. In addition, one hundred and five British missionaries had rendered fine service. Some of them gave of their labor and means for six months, some for one year, many for two years, and one elder for three and a half years.

The British Mission prospered and progressed during the war years. Our baptisms were almost on a par with the pre-war record. And finally, when the mission records were transferred to President Brown, there was a surplus of over eight thousand dollars in the mission funds—a small token toward the building of the temple in the British Isles, then (in 1944) only a cherished hope.

We asked the Lord for help, and we received intelligence—the light of truth—on how to solve, by obedience to his commandments, many of our mission and individual problems, and how to survive in faith and limb the crucial years of World War II.

Improvement Era, April 1969, pp. 60-63. Edited by compiler.

SATAN

The men and women who desire to obtain seats in the celestial kingdom will find that they must battle with the enemy of all righteousness every day.

—Brigham Young, *Journal of Discourses*, 11:14

THE PRINCE OF DARKNESS IS MINDFUL OF YOU
James Blaine Lindahl

I was still in my teens when I had a patriarchal blessing in which I was told of the choice blessings the Lord was holding in reserve for me if I would keep the commitments I had made in the pre-existence to serve him faithfully while here on earth. I was also told that the prince of darkness was also mindful of me and would attempt to lead me astray.

My only thoughts and concerns after I received my blessing were that I live my life in such a manner that I would be worthy of receiving the blessings that awaited me if I would faithfully serve the Lord. I was not overly apprehensive about the patriarch's pronouncement that the prince of darkness was mindful of me, as I was aware that the devil desires to lead *all* of Heavenly Father's children astray, so I felt no particular concern that I would be singled out for more than the usual consideration and attention by the adversary.

But I found out differently, just as soon as I made a commitment to my bishop to serve the Lord by going on a mission. I had always realized the great responsibilities one is given when he becomes a priesthood holder in our Heavenly Father's kingdom and is given the opportunity and responsibility of serving as a missionary. I felt that I should prepare myself a little more spiritually for the call that I was going to receive shortly, so this particular Friday night I decided to stay alone in my room in the Deseret Towers rather than take part in some of the social activities that night on the BYU campus. I spent the evening reading and on my knees praying, and felt as though I had really communicated with my Heavenly Father. It was a very spiritual evening—a time in which I had never felt as close to my Heavenly Father or so in tune with his spirit and desires for me.

I went to bed that night about 10:30 P.M., feeling at peace with myself and in complete harmony with the will of the Lord, and slept soundly until about 3:00 A.M. I awakened to feel a darkness beginning to come over me that quickly overpowered me, making me a prisoner to my bed. Immediately I realized what was happening to my body and the grave danger I was in, and tried to call for help, but found that I was unable to do so—my body was powerless to respond to my desires. I was greatly alarmed to find that I was unable to even open my mouth! Then panic set in as I suddenly realized that I was looking down at my own body lying on the bed!

A shadowy black form of a man was lying on top of me, trying to press in and take over my body. My soul recognized the gravity of the situation and immediately began to pray to the Lord for protection from the evil power. My spirit then began to realize that I must use the only power I possessed that could overcome this satanic spirit—the priesthood. I was only a priest at this time, but I knew that even in the Aaronic Priesthood I possessed a greater power than did the evil spirit that was taking over my body. So, I demanded, "In the name of Jesus Christ, will you leave?"

The power of darkness ignored my request and continued to press into my body. I repeated my demand again and again, but nothing happened! Finally, after about seven times of repeating the demand for him to leave in the name of the Savior, I found myself back in my bed, wringing wet from perspiration. I sat up in bed, delighted to be able to feel my body and know that my spirit and body were together again. After the joy of this discovery had passed and I began to reflect on what I thought I had experienced, I decided that it was all too ludicrous and was only a bad dream and had not really happened, so I went back to bed.

The second I lay back on my bed the experience repeated itself. This time I was wide awake and *very sure* of what was happening. I really was separated from my body and that same black form was moving over my body! This time, however, the spirit exerted even greater power and force over my body, so much so that I was fearful that unless something happened immediately I would surrender and surely die. At that moment, my soul began to cry out to the Lord Jesus Christ for protection, and I again repeatedly demanded that the evil spirit depart in the name of the Savior.

My cries to the Lord had awakened my roommate, who was greatly alarmed when he saw my situation. I was mumbling incoherently and thrashing around in my bed in such a violent manner as to leave little doubt in his mind that either I was possessed, or soon would be. He immediately ran down the hall to another apartment and got another elder to come and help him administer to me. They anointed me with oil and then tried to give me a blessing, but I was moving about so erratically that they found it difficult to keep their hands on my head. They commanded the evil spirit to depart, and I found myself back in my bed in a cold sweat and crying like a baby.

This experience so terrified me that I became very fearful of being alone in the dark, and even today, some four years later, I am still somewhat afraid of being alone.

Two weeks after this experience, I was ordained to the Melchizedek Priesthood and entered the Language Training Mission on the BYU campus. Often, during those lull times when I was not busy with my studies I would go into one of the unused rooms at the LTM and pray. Twice while I was on my knees praying I felt the presence of the adversary coming into the room and each time, with just one command in the name of the Lord Jesus Christ and the power of the Melchizedek Priesthood, the evil influence immediately departed. I was shaken by these experiences, literally, for I was shaking like a leaf when I related my experiences to the mission leader at the LTM. He warned me *never* to be alone, for the adversary was trying to overcome me. He also counselled me to tell my mission president in the mission field of my experiences with the adversary.

The president of the Uruguay-Paraguay Mission also warned me that I was to *always* stay with my companion and never be alone, because the devil was definitely trying to destroy me so that I could not fulfill this mission and the future missions and callings that were in store for me later in life.

I followed my mission president's advice and never was without the presence of a companion while I was in the mission field. I fulfilled a fruitful mission, and often felt the guiding influence of the Lord directing me in my work to bring my Latin-American brothers and sisters into the gospel. Occasionally, I felt the presence of the adversary working with some of our contacts, trying to keep them from joining the Church. The adversary has never made another attempt to destroy me since I left the LTM, nor do I expect him to in the future, for we both know that I now have the faith and the power to overcome him or any of his disciples he could send to destroy me.

During my mission and the three years since, I have developed a very strong testimony that the adversary will not have the power to overcome me if I will get down on my knees each night and pray to the Lord for his protection. The adversary is mindful of me, but so is the Lord.

GOD'S POWER MADE MANIFEST
President Heber J. Grant

When my wife died, I took my oldest three daughters to Boston, New York and other places in the hope that the sorrow caused by the death of their mother might be forgotten. When we reached Washington, two of them were taken ill with diphtheria. They were as sick as any children I have ever seen. The younger of the two was so low that her pulse beat only twenty-eight times to the minute, and I felt sure she was going to die. I knelt down and prayed God to spare her life, inasmuch as I had brought my children east to relieve the terrible sorrow that had come to them; and prayed that I should not have the additional sorrow of taking one of my children home in a coffin. I prayed for her life, and shed bitter tears of humiliation. While praying, the inspiration came to me that if I would send for the elders who were then in Washington and have them administer to her, she would live.

Some people may say we cannot know for a certainty that we receive manifestations from the Lord. Well, I know that I was shedding tears of sorrow, fear and anguish while I was praying, and I know that immediately thereafter I received the witness of the Spirit that my little girl should live, and I shed tears of unbounded joy and gratitude and thanksgiving to God, thanking him for the inspiration that came to me to send for the elders that they might administer to my little girl.

Hiram Clawson and George Q. Cannon were in Washington at the time, and I sent for them. When George Q. Cannon laid his hands upon my daughter's head to seal the anointing wherewith she had been anointed, he made a statement that I have never heard before or since, in all my life, in any prayer. He said in substance: "The adversary, the destroyer, has decreed your death and made public announcement that you shall die, but by the authority of the priesthood of the Living God, we rebuke the decree of the adversary, and say that you shall live, and not die; that you shall live to become a mother in the Church of Christ."

She did live to become a mother, and in the providences of the Lord her children are the great-grandchildren of the man who held the priesthood of God and gave her that blessing.

I often thought of that blessing during the days and weeks that she was convalescing, and I wondered about the peculiar statement that the adversary, the destroyer, had publicly announced her death. As we were leaving the boardinghouse, the gentleman whose wife had been in charge there—he was a clerk in one of the departments at Washington—said to me: "Mr. Grant, I have a joke on my wife. She believes in spiritualism, and when your little girls were taken sick she went to her medium." The medium went into a sort of trance and told her the following story:

That she saw two little girls in her house; she saw the older one taken sick, very sick; then the other little girl became sick, nigh unto death; she finally saw the first little girl recover and the second little girl die. She then described how the child's body was put into a coffin and taken to a railroad station; then she described how the train traveled, carrying the body of that little girl hundreds of miles to the west, through great cities, finally stopping in a large city where the body was transferred from one train to another. (Going from Washington you know that there is a transfer from all trains at Chicago.) Then she saw it cross two great rivers—the Missouri and the Mississippi, although not named —she afterward saw it traveling across the plains, and crossing mountains, mountains, mountains, always to the west, then saw it go south a little distance from Ogden to Salt Lake—although not giving the names—then the body was taken off the train and carried to a side hill to the place of burial; and as you know the burial place in Salt Lake City is on a side hill. But through the priesthood of the Living God, the decree of the adversary was rebuked, and my daughter lived.

Deseret News, April 24, 1920.

POWER OF THE ADVERSARY
President Heber J. Grant

Upon one occasion Wilford Woodruff went to a place where spiritualistic meetings had been held for many weeks. Brother Woodruff went there as a missionary, after having prayed to the Living God that he would shut up the shop, figuratively speaking, of the spiritualistic medium.

An audience of about three hundred people had assembled, and the medium was prepared to give his lecture and his spiritualistic demonstration, as he had been doing on former occasions; but he found it impossible to proceed with the usual manifestations. He jumped down from the platform, walked around through the aisles, here and there among the audience, and finally came to Brother Woodruff. Shaking his fist in Brother Woodruff's face, he said: "You are the man who is keeping me from doing anything tonight!"

Brother Woodruff said: "Yes, I am the fellow. I am here with the priesthood of the Living God, and I have rebuked the power of the adversary. You can't do anything while I am here!"

After a while the audience asked Brother Woodruff to please withdraw, and he did so; and they had the devil's own time after he left.

Deseret News, April 24, 1920.

HANDLED BY THE DEVIL
Philo Dibble

At this time (1831) Sidney Rigdon was left to preside at Kirtland and frequently preached to us. Upon one occasion he said the keys of the kingdom were taken from us. On hearing this, many of his hearers wept; and when someone undertook to dismiss the meeting by prayer, he said praying would do them no good, and the meeting broke up in confusion.

Brother Hyrum came to my house the next morning and told me all about it, and said it was false, and that the keys of the kingdom were still with us. He wanted my carriage and horses to go to the town of Hiram and bring Joseph. The word went abroad among the people immediately that Sidney was going to expose Mormonism.

Joseph came up to Kirtland a few days afterwards and held a meeting in a large barn. Nearly all the inhabitants of Kirtland turned out to hear him. The barn was filled with people, and others, unable to get inside, stood around the door as far as they could hear.

Joseph arose in our midst and spoke in mighty power, saying, "I can contend with wicked men and devils—yes with angels. No power can pluck those keys from me, except the power that gave them to me; that was Peter, James, and John. But for what Sidney has done, the devil shall handle him as one man handles another."

Thomas B. Marsh's wife went from the meeting and told Sidney what Joseph had said, and he replied, "Is it possible that I have been so deceived? But if Joseph says so, it is so."

About three weeks after this, Sidney was lying on his bed alone. An unseen power lifted him from his bed, threw him across the room, and tossed him from one side of the room to the other. The noise being heard in the adjoining room, his family went in to see what was the matter, and found him going from one side of the room to the other, the effects of which laid Sidney up for five or six weeks. Thus was Joseph's prediction in regard to him verified.

"Philo Dibble's Narrative," *Early Scenes in Church History* (Eighth book of the Faith-Promoting Series, Salt Lake City: Juvenile Instructor Office, 1882), pp. 79-80.

A CONCERT BY THE ADVERSARY
Solomon F. Kimball

The most remarkable experiences that I ever passed through occurred during the nine years that I lived in Arizona. The first event of importance took place in October, 1877.

After crossing a seventy-five-mile desert with ox teams, my spiritual ears were opened, to my sorrow. From eleven o'clock at night until daylight the next morning, while driving our jaded animals up a sandy wash in search of water, I listened to a satanic string band that caused every fiber in my dejected body to quiver. The deep, doleful, lonesome sound almost drove me wild, while my swollen tongue was protruding from my burning mouth. Every part of that horrible dirge was perfectly played, interpreting, most excellently, the terrible ordeal through which I was passing, causing my mind to suffer more intensely than my body, if such a thing were possible.

Those dismal sounds rumble in my ears to this day, causing me to shudder when I think of it!

Solomon F. Kimball, "Spiritual-Mindedness," *Life of David P. Kimball* (Salt Lake City: The Deseret News, 1918), pp. 101-102.

EVIL PRESENCE IN A WINTER NIGHT
Esther Heaton Lamb

I loved winter days, but this one was, without evident cause, filled with depression. I looked around our small homestead home, sensing its tidiness and comfort. With the house all seemed well. It glowed from the brightness of the warming fire behind the hearth.

I looked from the window, observing the muddy road that led down a long street, turned at the creek and went on to my mother's house. The gentle three-day rain had soaked to overflowing our thirsty land. To me the day was not dreary, but clean-aired and lovely.

Maybe this unease that frightened me was due to loneliness because my husband, Earl, was away, and had been for several months. Yes, I did miss him but I felt that this unidentified worry was not about him.

Just then, from the old-fashioned cradle that had rocked my mother's children in their infancy, and now held my first-born son, came a choking gasp that seemed to stifle the very life from him.

Fear tripped the rhythmic beat of my heart. He had always been a strong, healthy child. Somehow I knew that this first hoarse cry was a warning of something more to be dreaded than the croup. Taking him in my arms, I did all I knew how to do to relieve his congestion. I soon realized that my knowledge was insufficient to cope with an unnamed force that had taken possession of my home.

Wrapping my three-year-old daughter Rua in a coat and putting on her boots, I took her to the porch. "You know where Grandma Heaton lives?" I asked her quietly. "Can you find your way there alone?"

She nodded her head.

"Will you go as quickly as you can and tell Grandma that we need her here? Be very careful crossing the creek and the wash bridges."

Fear was evident in her eyes, yet she did not hesitate. Returning to the inside of the house, I stood by the window, holding the sick baby and prayerfully watching my tiny girl disappear into the haze of rain. How I loved her.

"Telephone," you say. Only the general store had one. "A car?" We had none. "Doctor?" None.

I knew a deep thankfulness when I saw my mother emerge from the mist, holding tightly to Rua's hand.

All day and far into the night we worked and prayed. At times the tension eased and we felt encouraged, only to be torn again by a worsening of the situation. At three o'clock in the morning the evil one added to his presence a definite desire. Each breath drawn by the baby was more difficult than the one before and the color of life left his body. Fear is a word we use because no other is better to describe it. Mother and I experienced its meaning far beyond any word. Even Rua was uneasy as she slept.

Everyone at some time in their life knows the death of loved ones—the sorrow, the despair, and later the comfort. We knew that with us that night was a power of destruction that we had never experienced before.

"We must have help," I whispered to mother, afraid to even speak the reason aloud. Yet I knew she understood and felt as I did. My heart almost burst with love for her.

She said, "Will you go for Uncle Ed (Carroll) or shall I?"

Afraid to stay without her, but also afraid my baby would die while I was away, I asked her to go.

My little mother ran the mile to town, awakened Uncle Ed and was back ahead of him. The minute he stepped onto our porch, the baby's breathing eased and normal color returned to his face. Uncle Ed greeted me cheerfully, sat long enough to warm himself by the fire, then blessed the resting baby.

After a while of pleasant chatting, Uncle Ed said, "It is almost morning, and the baby seems all right. I will be going."

The words *thank you* seemed too small for expressing the relief he gave us when he came and lifted the burden of fear from our hearts.

He stepped off the porch and walked away, and our battle began again. Fearfully we watched the baby's fight for life. Even as he grew weaker, we prayed to add strength to the blessing he had received. Could it be that we were to say, "Thy will be done" and give back to Him our little son? Mother and I felt distinctly that the power or will that was in the house that night was not of the Lord.

When morning came, I ran to the highway, waited for someone to pass by, and sent a message to Uncle Ed. He came immediately. At once, with certain authority, he blessed the baby. He rebuked and cast from our presence the evil one who for twenty-four hours had contended with us for the life of my child.

At once complete freedom came. The baby was restored and we knew that the power of God, through a worthy member of his priesthood, had overcome Satan.

Gwen Heaton Sherratt and Hannah Heaton Roundy, *Esther's Children* (William Heaton Family Organization, 1966), pp. 206-207.

TEMPLE WORK

You hold the keys of the destiny of your fathers, your mothers, your progenitors, from generation to generation; you hold the keys of their salvation. God has put that power into your hands. But if we do not do what is required of us in this thing, we are under condemnation. If we do attend to this, when we come to meet our friends in the celestial kingdom, they will say, "You have been our saviors, because you had power to do it. You have attended to these ordinances that God has required."

—Wilford Woodruff, *Conference Report,* October 1897, p. 38

SAGA OF SACRIFICE
Richard J. Marshall

Former President, Australia West Mission

What sacrifices would you be willing to make to go to the temple? Would you sell your car? Jeopardize your home? Give up your job?

These thoughts nagged at the mind of the young district president, Donald W. Cummings, of Perth, Australia. The mission president had challenged the Australian Saints to attend the New Zealand Temple dedication, just four months—but four thousand miles—away. Perth was the farthest district from Church headquarters—so far that if you went any farther you would be heading back to Zion.

The mission president's challenge kept ringing in his ears: "If you have a righteous goal and pray about it, the Lord will help you achieve it."

President Cummings reviewed his finances. He was struggling to purchase a home for his burgeoning family; he earned only a modest salary; he had no money in the bank; he drove an old car. The price of going to New Zealand was six hundred pounds (twelve hundred U. S. dollars). He set his jaw and picked up the newspaper to look in the classified section for loans.

Several years earlier, every Melchizedek Priesthood holder in the district, including Donald Cummings, had driven three thousand miles round trip, much of it on primitive dirt roads, in two battered cars, to see President David O. McKay during his historic visit to Adelaide, South Australia. Now President Cummings was twenty-six years old, a convert of ten years and district president for eight months over an area that encompassed the entire state of Western Australia, nearly one million square miles.

He began preparations for their temple trip. He borrowed money on his furniture, the last loan of that type granted by the company. He sold the car and started walking, riding buses, even hitchhiking. And, during the next eighteen months, he never missed his visits to any branch. He recalls, "Yes, it was hard getting around, but my wife and I remember this as one of the happiest periods of our lives. We had discovered the joys of sacrifice for the Lord. We appreciated walking all the more."

Even after selling the car and mortgaging both house and furniture, he was still two hundred dollars short—with no other funds in sight and only a few weeks to go. President Cummings had to give his company notice, for they would not hold his job open for six weeks.

With less than a week to go, a relative who was not a member of the Church met him on the street and surprised him with a gift of one hundred dollars. With one day left before departure, another nonmember relative drove in from the country and pressed the final one hundred dollars into his hands. President and Sister Cummings both knew that "the Lord had intervened. He had touched the hearts of those closest to us."

The eight-thousand-mile round trip started with a two-thousand-mile, four-and-a-half-day train ride across the width of the Australian outback. In Sydney, the family delightedly met with the other Saints who had also arranged passage on a boat bound for Auckland.

To their wrenching disappointment, the boat had just been damaged in hitting the wharf, but remarkably, they were able to charter an airplane without any excess cost. They all flew to the dedication and witnessed this sacred event as President David O. McKay presided and prayed. President Cummings spoke in the spacious auditorium of the new Church College adjacent to the temple. The family was blessed to attend the first day of endowments; they were also members of the first company to do work for the dead.

The Cummings family planned to lodge in tents, for their funds were so meager. But at the last minute, arrangements were made for hotel accommodations. They would pay later—but they were never billed, nor could they discover whom to pay. Too poor to tour, they rejoiced in working in the temple for several weeks. Then, filled with the spirit of their new blessings, they traveled home with ten dollars in their pockets, no job, no car, and mortgages on their home and furniture. But they were rich in rewards that only a temple can provide: they were sealed together for time and eternity.

President Cummings went back to his old employer and to his astonishment was hired as a sales manager with an increase in pay. But he would not get paid until the end of the week, and their money had run out completely. There was nothing to eat. One of his wife's country relatives paid a surprise visit and dropped off enough fresh garden produce to sustain them until payday.

When Elder Thomas S. Monson of the Council of the Twelve organized the Perth Stake in 1968, Donald W. Cummings became its first president. He had seen the kingdom of God swell from a handful to a stake, but he never forgot the promise of his mission president: "If you have a righteous goal and pray about it, the Lord will help you achieve it."

Ensign, August 1974, pp. 66-67.

YOU MISSED THAT NAME
James Blaine Lindahl

While attending BYU, I had the choice privilege of assisting in the vicarious work for the dead at the nearby Provo Temple. With the utilization of technological advances we were able to perform the baptisms for over eight hundred people in one session, which is about one name every seven seconds. The recorder's list of names of those individuals whose work is to be performed is projected via television camera onto a small television in view of the individual doing the baptizing. This eliminates the necessity for the recorder to repeat the name to the person baptizing, and also eliminates the possibility of the name being misunderstood.

This particular session, I was the one in the font performing the baptisms. The session was progressing as usual when the brother who escorts the group to the font and who was seated some distance from the recorder suddenly left his seat and went to the recorder's side. This is *never* done, as no one is supposed to be close enough to the recorder to distract him from complete concentration on his list of names. Pointing to a name on the list, the witness stated, "You missed that name!"

An immediate check was made and we found that somehow that particular name had been inadvertently pulled through the camera viewing area without the recorder and me having seen it. We had both assumed that all the people whose names appeared on our list had been baptized, which meant that the individual whose name we missed would probably have had to wait until the millennium to be baptized, because of a human error. We were, of course, very grateful to have had this oversight pointed out to us and immediately corrected the situation by performing the baptism for the individual whose name we had omitted.

I have a firm conviction and strong testimony that those departed souls that have accepted the gospel in the spirit world and desire baptism are present in the temple when their long-awaited work is done, for I have felt their presence. I also feel that there was no possible way the witness could have known that one name had been missed, unless he had been prompted by some spirit— perhaps the spirit of the man whose baptism was not done.

LUCIFER TRIES TO HINDER TEMPLE WORK
Elder Rudger Clawson

On one occasion I heard the late apostle Marriner W. Merrill, president of the Logan Temple, relate this extraordinary incident:

He was sitting in his office one morning, he said, when he noticed from the window a company of people coming up the hill to the temple. As they entered the temple grounds, they presented rather a strange appearance, not only in dress but in their mode of travel. Some were riding horses, others were in conveyances, and still others were afoot. He wondered who they could be, as he was not looking for a company of such size that particular morning. They dismounted from their horses, stepped down from their conveyances, put their animals under the shade and walked about complacently as if they had a perfect right to be there.

A little later a person unknown to Brother Merrill entered the room. Brother Merrill said to him, "Who are you and who are these people who have come up and taken possession of the temple grounds unannounced?" He answered and said, "I am Satan and these are my people."

Brother Merrill then said, "What do you want? Why have you come here?"

Satan replied, "I don't like the work that is going on in this temple and feel that it should be discontinued. Will you stop it?"

Brother Merrill answered and said emphatically, "No, we will not stop it! The work must go on!"

"Since you refuse to stop it, I will tell you what I propose to do," the adversary said. "I will take these people, my followers, and distribute them throughout this temple district, and will instruct them to whisper in the ears of the people, persuading them not to go to the temple, and thus bring about a cessation of your temple work." Satan then withdrew.

President Merrill, commenting on this strange interview with the evil one, said that for quite a period of time the spirit of indifference to temple work seemed to take possession of the people and very few came to the house of the Lord. The presumption was that Satan had carried out his threat, which caused a temporary lull in temple work.